P9-APW-823

THE NATIONAL DEBT
CONCLUSION

THE NATIONAL DEBT CONCLUSION

Establishing the Debt Repayment Plan

CHARLES W. STEADMAN

PRAEGER

Westport, Connecticut
London

The author acknowledges William Mark Crain, whose exceptional talents and devoted assistance were invaluable in the production of this book.

Library of Congress Cataloging-in-Publication Data

Steadman, Charles W.
    The national debt conclusion : establishing the debt repayment plan
  / Charles W. Steadman.
        p.   cm.
    Includes bibliographical references and index.
    ISBN 0-275-94360-7 (alk. paper)
    1. Debts, Public—United States.   2. United States—Economic
  policy. I. Title.
  HJ8101.S74   1993
  336.3′4′0973—dc20   92-44688

British Library Cataloguing in Publication Data is available.

Library of Congress Catalog Card Number: 92-44688
ISBN: 0-275-94360-7

First published in 1993

Praeger Publishers, 88 Post Road West, Westport, CT 06881
An imprint of Greenwood Publishing Group, Inc.

Printed in the United States of America

The paper used in this book complies with the Permanent Paper Standard issued by the National Information Standards Organization (Z39.48-1984).

10 9 8 7 6 5 4 3 2

To Consuelo, my wife,
joy of my life and
treasure of my soul.

Contents

Figures and Tables

FIGURES

THE NATIONAL DEBT
CONCLUSION

1

National Debt:
The Greater Force and
Dictator of Policy

As a very important source of strength and
security, cherish public credit. One method of
preserving it is to use it as sparingly as possible;
avoid occasions of expense by cultivating peace,
but remembering also that timely disbursements to
prepare for danger frequently prevent much
greater disbursements to repel it; avoid likewise
the accumulation of debt, not only by shunning
occasions of expense, but by vigorous exertions in
time of peace to discharge the debts which
unavoidable wars may have occasioned, not
ungenerously throwing upon posterity the burdens
which we ourselves ought to bear.[1]

—George Washington

General Washington wisely identified economic power as
the basis of a nation's position of strength in the world.
Then, as now, a nation's position in the world is predicated
upon economic power. And a nation's preeminence among
other nations is predicated upon an ability to impose by
means of force those propositions which function to achieve

and maintain its best interests. That force is wealth which when translated into a mercantile concept provides for domination of trade and creation of wealth, and when translated into a military concept provides for the protection and acquisition of wealth.

What was clear to the Founders and those who succeeded them through many generations of building America's resources atrophied in the New Deal. Deficits are everywhere we look and the accumulating national debt threatens America's preeminence in the twenty-first century. Yet the problem has been buried under the political rug and consequently without forthright attention programs for expenditures continue to rise to eclipse revenue and devour surpluses actual or anticipated. In fiscal year 1992, the national debt reached $4 trillion. This number is so large that it seems almost meaningless, but it is quite real and a serious danger to the stability of the social order within the United States.

We borrow money to maintain a standard of living that is beyond our present productive capacity. We do not work hard enough nor produce and sell enough to support this standard of living. In other words we are not earning enough to pay for our life-style. So we charge it and hand the bills to our children and grandchildren. We drain off domestic savings and strain our credit abroad by an endless selling and refunding of Treasury securities. The pool of domestic savings is not sufficient to finance federal spending at present levels. By many measures the United States is broke. And if foreigners stop buying Treasury issues, the federal government's choice will be default or drastic reduction of spending.

By some estimates the standard of living in the United States, beginning in the 1990s, will have declined by as much as 10 percent *for each American* as a consequence of the debt accumulated during the 1980s alone. The United States collectively consumed nearly a trillion dollars in products it did not pay for (the budget deficits) or did not produce (the international trade deficits). The growth rate in output in the

1990s is progressing on a basis of less than 1 percent annually. This is less than the increase in the population and will not support any improvement in living standards. Indeed, a lowering of the standard of living under these conditions will prevail indefinitely.

The debt burden does more than gradually reduce American's standard of living; it represents a straight-jacket that constrains government's ability to deal effectively with problems at home and abroad. The debt dictates policy options. The decline of national wealth caused by the debt burden is steadily eroding America's sovereignty and global influence. In the absence of an appropriate plan for its retirement the debt will in the years ahead relentlessly undermine our democratic institutions and social order.

American's are drowning in debt, about which there is much posturing and hand-wringing in the political arena. But as of yet there has been very little hard thinking about why we should be concerned not only about the size of the *deficit* but also about the size of the *debt*. We are in a public debt trap from which we must devise an escape.

A political process unable to resolve the debt crisis is in dire need of structural reform and a rational initiative to reverse decades of federal fiscal profligacy. This book develops a Plan for national debt retirement that is sensitive to political considerations and economic realities. The Plan is supported by empirical experience as shown in past cases of successful debt repayment and by the certain decline of American preeminence under the prevailing course of fiscal policy.

Chapter 2 examines the causes for growth in the national debt. Chapter 3 turns to the consequences of a large and growing debt from a macro perspective. How the debt disrupts the important interdependent relationships between saving, investment, productivity, and income are addressed. Chapter 4 illuminates how the debt is managed and serviced and focuses on the problems that result from the practice of continuous debt refunding. Chapters 5 and 6 analyze the impact of national debt on the average American and on future generations. Chapter 7 examines the promise and short-comings of national fiscal policies from the Carter through the Bush administrations. Chapters 8 and 9 evaluate the historical experience of the United States with debt repayment after its various wars, from the Revolutionary War to World War II. Chapter 10 presents a proposal for retiring the national debt. The Epilogue concludes with two visions of the future. One assumes the continuation of business as usual for another decade; the other assumes the implementation of the Plan for Debt Retirement.

NOTE

[1]Committee on Public Debt Policy, *Our National Debt* (New York: Harcourt, Brace and Co.), pp. 21–22.

2

Why Has the National Debt Grown?

Discovering a cure for the national debt would be far easier if we had a clear grasp of its underlying causes. Until the mid-twentieth century a considerable portion of the then current national debt arose from the financing of several wars.[1] In order to finance these wars, Congress could have voted to avoid any new debts by raising taxes to cover the cost entirely, but taxation is not a popular measure even while war is in progress and certainly not otherwise. Thus, the United States has financed its wars in part by borrowing and in part by raising taxes. But most importantly, the debts incurred during wartime were repaid, and repaid relatively quickly until the years following World War II.

In the second half of the twentieth century there was a change of course. The policy of debt repayment was superceded and the result was a near doubling of the debt in relation to the nation's economy in the 1970s and 1980s. At one level this persistent debt is quite easy to explain: federal government expenditures simply grew faster than federal revenues. But this only states the result and not the cause. It fails to explain why the national debt became a permanent fixture in the post-World War II period but not previously.

The seeds of America's modern debt dilemma began to

germinate in the early twentieth century, the product of a combination of factors that created a fertile environment for the debt to flourish and become increasingly resistant to eradication. We begin discovery with a probe of the pertinent facts.

SURRENDERING CONTROL OVER THE POWER TO TAX

> The Congress shall have the power to lay and collect taxes on incomes, from whatever source derived, without apportionment among the several States, and without regard to any census or enumeration.
>
> —United States Constitution, Amendment XVI

The Sixteenth Amendment was ratified on February 25, 1913 as part of the Constitution, amending Article 1 and thereby granting Congress the power to lay and collect taxes on income without apportionment and "without regard to any census or enumeration." This amendment directly overruled a 1895 Supreme Court decision that an income tax was unconstitutional on the grounds that it violated Article 1, Section 9, Clause 4 of the Constitution:[2] "No Capitulation, or other direct Tax shall be laid, unless in Proportion to the Census or Enumeration herein before directed to be taken."

The authority to impose income taxes provided the federal government with power to manipulate and transfer wealth from one group to another and gave it dominion over the economy to an extent not theretofore possible or envisioned by the Founding Fathers.[3] This radical expansion of federal power made possible the New Deal spending programs enacted during the 1930s under President Franklin Roosevelt's administration amidst the turmoil of a severe economic depression. Between 1929 and 1939 federal spending grew from 2.5 percent of gross national product (GNP) to 9.8 percent, roughly a four-fold increase in a single decade. The Sixteenth Amendment lodged within the domain of the federal government a right which the Framers had never intended it to have. This right to impose "direct" taxes on personal and corporate earnings, which vastly expanded the federal government's taxing authority, opened a flood gate through which federal spending flowed. And with these programs came federal intervention into the economic and social affairs of the nation that would become increasingly difficult to restrain. Federalism was destroyed, and these United States as a republic were swept into the past.

The growing inability to control federal spending which is at the core of the modern debt problem has roots that trace to the surrender of unbridled taxing authority to the federal government. With more power to tax came more power to borrow as the federal government's capacity to raise future revenues was enormously expanded. Lenders were thus more willing to supply the credit necessary to fund federal programs because the enhanced tax base provided collateral with which their loans were secured. Increased federal borrowing in the flurry of Roosevelt's New Deal raised the national debt from 16 percent of GNP in 1929 to 44 percent in 1939. During the next decade, with the entry of the United States into World War II and the subsequent United States financed Marshall Plan to assist in the rebuilding of Europe, the national debt reached 98 percent of GNP. (In 1946 the debt as a percentage of GNP reached 128 percent, still its highest level in United States history.)

Following World War II the nation had lost its enthusiasm for paying off a debt that was roughly equivalent to a full year of its entire national output. Government assistance programs born in the New Deal era created political constituencies that were eager to continue receiving transfer payments from the government upon which they had come to depend. And politicians did not want to risk defeat by denying these privileges. Why were taxes not increased to finance these spending programs? Federal tax revenues during the 1930s and 1940s were in fact dramatically increased. As a share of GNP, revenues doubled from 3.7 percent in 1929 to 7.4 percent in 1939. From 1939 to 1949 they doubled again, rising to 15 percent. Having felt the tax burden quadruple within a single generation, voters were strongly adverse to the even further increases that would have been necessary to keep pace with run-away federal spending.

Borrowing was thus a less painful political alternative than the denial of constituent benefits or further increases in the tax burden.

PERVERSE RULES OF THE FISCAL POLICY GAME

Reasons of political philosophy dedicated to restricting the authority of the newly to be created central government led the Constitution writers to an explicit prohibition on the general taxing authority of Congress, in contrast to power as exercised by the British government under George III. This prohibition was reversed in the twentieth century and taxing power of the federal government became subject only to electoral restraint. The Treasury became open for political self-perpetuation. This comprehension is that paramount to understanding growth of the national debt. Fiscal policy is not determined in a political vacuum, but rather is the outcome of the democratic-electoral process. And the democratic process is, in turn, defined by the rules and constraints which confront elected officials whose success is measured at the ballot box.

This illustration will be useful. Suppose that within a polity of 100 citizens, a ten-member coalition demands a program that will cost $1,000. This program can be thought of as a pure transfer program whereby each coalition member receives an equal $100 share. To pay for this transfer program suppose the government levies a direct $10 tax on all citizens. The consequences of this arrangement are quite predictable. The program's $1,000 benefits are concentrated within a relatively small constituent group, whereas the program's costs are widely dispersed. The *pro rata* benefits, $100, are substantial in relation to the $10 *pro rata* taxes. The incentive for the beneficiary group to lobby and to provide electoral support for legislators who favor their transfer program outweighs by a factor of 10 the incentive of disorganized taxpayers to oppose the plan.

The moral of this elementary example is that the democratic process is not perfect: programs that are not in the interest of the majority can be enacted if supported by an intensely interested minority. Policy decisions are sensitive to the incentives and constraints within which legislators are allowed to choose. Of particular relevance is the effect of a constraint on Congress, or the absence thereof, to impose generalized tax levies. The Founding Fathers apparently realized the incentive problem inherent in allowing Congress the authority to finance programs with generalized taxes. The potential for Congress to tax the many for the benefit of a few could otherwise proceed unchecked.

Only a small leap is needed for the extension of this logic to incentives for financing spending programs by borrowing rather than taxing. The costs borne by the citizenry from borrowing are no less real than the costs from direct taxation. Yet, not infrequently the eventual costs of borrowing are even more dispersed among the citizens — future as well as present — than direct taxation. That some of the costs from government borrowing are not as readily recognizable as the more obvious costs from taxes also infuses an even stronger political motivation to enact spending programs financed by borrowing rather than those financed by the proceeds of taxation.[4]

The adoption of the Sixteenth Amendment, which radically changed the Constitutional rules governing fiscal policy, was itself a product of interest group efforts to redistribute wealth. The relatively poor states of the Southern and Western United States stood to gain from an income tax because its burden would fall primarily upon the then wealthier Northeastern states. It was in this context that Senators and Representatives from the South and West in 1909 were successful in enacting the resolution required to send the proposed amendment to the states for ratification. Expectedly the 36 states that eventually voted to ratify the amendment were in the South and West as Table 2-1 illustrates. The Northeastern states were likewise a united opposition. This Constitutional action was not a shining example of politics that promotes the general welfare or the national interest. It was the rawest form of interest group politics. And the social and economic consequences for America's future must not be underestimated: massive government programs to manipulate and redistribute wealth, special interest politics, the denigration of savings, and the eventual forfeiture of

TABLE 2-1

RATIFICATION HISTORY OF THE SIXTEENTH AMENDMENT*

State **	Ratification Date	State **	Ratification Date
Alabama	Aug. 10, 1909	North Carolina	Feb. 11, 1911
Kentucky	Feb. 8, 1910	Colorado	Feb. 15, 1911
South Carolina	Feb. 19, 1910	North Dakota	Feb. 17, 1911
Illinois	Mar. 1, 1910	Kansas	Feb. 18, 1911
Mississippi	Mar. 7, 1910	Michigan	Feb. 23, 1911
Oklahoma	Mar. 10, 1910	Iowa	Feb. 24, 1911
Maryland	Apr. 8, 1910	Missouri	Mar. 16, 1911
Georgia	Aug. 3, 1910	Maine	Mar. 31, 1911
Texas	Aug. 16, 1910	Tennessee	Apr. 7, 1911
Ohio	Jan. 19, 1911	Arkansas	Apr. 22, 1911
Idaho	Jan. 20, 1911	Wisconsin	May 26, 1911
Oregon	Jan. 23, 1911	New York	Jul. 12, 1911
Washington	Jan. 26, 1911	Arizona	Apr. 6, 1912
Montana	Jan. 30, 1911	Minnesota	Jun. 11, 1912
Indiana	Jan. 30, 1911	Louisiana	Jun. 28, 1912
California	Jan. 31, 1911	West Virginia	Jan. 31, 1913
Nevada	Jan. 31, 1911	Delaware	Feb. 3, 1913
South Dakota	Feb. 3, 1911	Wyoming	Feb. 3, 1913
Nebraska	Feb. 9, 1911	New Mexico	Feb. 3, 1913

* Text of Amendment: "The Congress shall have power to lay and collect taxes on incomes, from whatever source derived, without apportionment among the several States, and without regard to any census or enumeration.

** At the time there were 48 states in the Union; 36 were required to ratify.

controlling growth of the national debt.

LORD KEYNES AND OTHER ACADEMIC SCRIBBLERS

Several writers have argued persuasively that a paradigm shift in economics spawned by the theories of British economist John Maynard Keynes was a major factor behind the emergence of deficit-financed government spending. Keynesian ideology champions the thesis that economies, in the absence of government intervention, could under certain conditions fall into a permanent state of high unemployment, excess capacity, and declining real incomes. Government spending to supplement inadequate levels of private sector expenditures is then needed to raise profits, stimulate new investment, and revitalize economic expansion. However, government spending to stimulate expansions, Keynes concluded, should not be paid for by tax increases that would reduce incomes and thus private consumption even further. Keynesian ideology with its aversion to a tax increase in these circumstances prescribes borrowing to finance government programs as a policy solution during periods of major economic decline. It became a perfect foil for politicians to rationalize what they wanted to do anyway: use the public purse to win elections.

COMMENTARY

The national debt escaped control in the early 1990s, the result of a political process driven by short-term horizons and efforts to defer costs until after the next elections. Institutional rules that at one time guarded against perverse fiscal policies were eliminated, most notably the repeal of the Constitutional prohibition on income taxes. The Sixteenth Amendment paved the way for government programs to grow and made borrowing the most painless way to support the demands of the interest groups dependent on wealth transfers brokered by the federal government. And elected officials depend upon their ability to broker such transfers in exchange for votes. The nation came into the grip of a determination to redistribute wealth by use of a tax system in the hands of the federal government which made political self-perpetuation a reality.

NOTES

[1]The handling of the national debt prior to World War II is covered more extensively in Chapters 8 and 9.

[2]The case was *Pollock v. Farmers' Loan and Trust Company*, 157 U.S. 429 (1895) and 158 U.S. 601 (1895). For further historical discussion, see Committee on the Judiciary, U.S. Senate, *Amendments to the Constitution: A Brief Legislative History*, Washington, DC: U.S. Government Printing Office, October 1985.

[3]Before the Civil War, tariffs, duties, and excise taxes normally supplied adequate revenue for the operation of the federal government. However, with an increasing national debt in the 1850s and with the added expense of the Civil War during the 1860s, Congress enacted a temporary income tax to alleviate the federal financial burden. This Civil War income tax continued until 1872 when Congress allowed it to expire.

[4]The costs of public debt are examined more fully in Chapters 4, 5, and 6.

3

Sacrifice of Opportunity

Indications that the long-term vitality of the United States economy was in jeopardy appeared in the 1980s, despite the fact that personal consumption expenditures continued to grow at about the same pace that they had in the 1970s.[1] The consumption spree many Americans were enjoying in the 1980s, however, was supported not by growing productivity, but rather was achieved at the expense of declining investment and from an influx of borrowed foreign savings. This condition could not prevail indefinitely. Economic prosperity is ultimately constrained by a nation's ability to produce, and the ability of a nation to produce is determined by the creation of capital.

The downward slide in America's investment in productive capacity and its living standards are inexorably connected to the increasingly large overhang of national debt. Excessive federal borrowing drains the pool of national savings and preempts resources that might otherwise be used to finance investments and technological innovations. The slowdown in investment activity lowers the productivity of American workers and, in turn, family incomes decline. With incomes declining, the ability of American's to save is further reduced, leaving fewer resources available for investment. How the national debt disrupts the important interdependent relationships between saving, investment, productivity, and income will be discussed.

FEDERAL BORROWING AS A DRAIN ON NATIONAL SAVING

The pool of national savings underwrites all forms of debt, ranging from United States Treasury securities to corporate borrowing to home mortgages to family credit cards. The federal government must borrow to finance deficit spending by putting Treasury securities up for auction. The federal government is then a borrower in competition with other borrowers in the private and public sectors seeking funds out of the national savings pool.

This national savings pool thus provides the most reliable measure of the debt load the nation can handle without putting undesirable upward pressure on interest rates. This measure is not typically used, however. Instead, the size of the deficit in relation to the nation's total output (for example gross national product [GNP] or gross domestic product [GDP]) is the most commonly used indicator of the potential for federal borrowing to drive up interest rates and impede economic growth. But measures that compare federal borrowing against GNP or GDP are misleading. Neither GNP nor GDP is a dependable guide because they include resources devoted to a host of functions that are irrelevant for investment purposes.[2]

Figure 3-1 illustrates the size of the federal deficit in relation to personal domestic savings since 1970. During the 1970s, the deficit as a percentage of personal savings averaged 38 percent. During the 1980s the average climbed to 88 percent and hit 121 percent in 1991. The significance of this is that federal deficits totally absorbed the United States domestic savings pool in the early 1990s and more. As this indicator boldly reveals, in the absence of either (or both) reduced federal spending or increased taxes, borrowing from international sources offered the only possible way to support continued federal spending and borrowing.

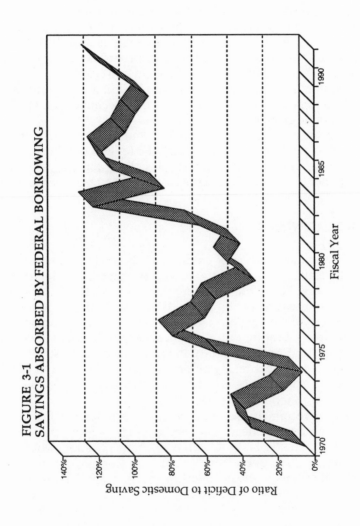

FIGURE 3-1
SAVINGS ABSORBED BY FEDERAL BORROWING

As the most creditworthy of borrowers, the federal government has always obtained what it needs to finance the
deficit, but in taking what it needs for deficit financing, less
of the savings pool is available from which others could
draw. As the share of the nation's savings absorbed by the
federal government deficits grows progressively larger, the
well of remaining resources begins to run dry. Private
investors are then preempted from building new plants and
machinery and from developing new technologies vital to
economic growth.

By increasing the competition among borrowers for the
limited pool of national savings, the federal debt pushes up
interest rates. And as interest rates climb some investments
will not be undertaken as the cost of money becomes prohib-
itively high.[3]

BORROWING FOR WHAT?

The vital function of credit markets is to channel savings
into activities that create new productive capacity in the
economy. Borrowing is a necessary part of this process and
does not reduce wealth per se. When debt is incurred for the
purpose of creating a productive asset — a new machine for
example — future output is increased and incomes will be
higher, and thus the ability to repay the debt is established.
Indebtedness becomes a problem when the borrowed funds
are not used for productivity-enhancing purposes, but instead are used for consumption activities.[4]

If government spending behind the federal deficit were
flowing into public investment activities — as it has at times
in the nation's history — the relevant question would be
whether these public investments are more productive than
the alternative private investments that are foregone. The
nation, in that case, would be trading off government
financed investments for privately financed investments. But
this question is practically irrelevant because most of the
funds borrowed by the federal government are used to
finance consumption activities, not public investments.
Figure 3-2 illustrates the downward trend in federal
spending on investments.[5] The nation is substituting public

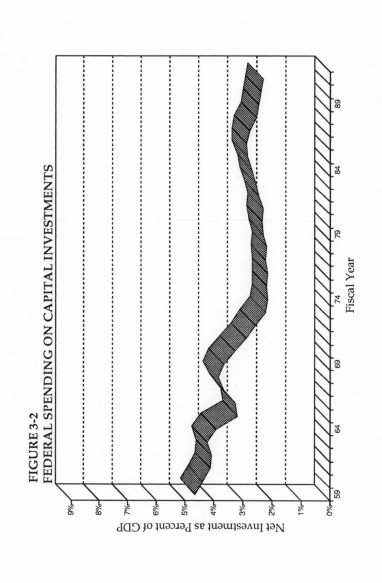

FIGURE 3-2
FEDERAL SPENDING ON CAPITAL INVESTMENTS

Net Investment as Percent of GDP

Fiscal Year

consumption for private investment.

DEBT AS A BARRIER TO CAPITAL FORMATION

The struggle to channel the national savings pool into the creation of capital is being lost as Figure 3-3 illustrates. In the 1960s net private investment represented 6.3 percent of GDP; in the 1980s it had fallen to 5.4 percent. In 1991 only 1.8 percent of the nation's output was channeled into new investments.

These low and declining levels of investment in the United States are directly linked to the large and rising levels of the national debt. As the debt absorbs the nation's savings it exerts upward pressure on interest rates. And as interest rates climb, the costs of funds for constructing new plants and equipment become more expensive and, naturally, fewer productive projects will be undertaken.

A second and perhaps more subtle link between the debt and capital formation should be stressed as well. The large national debt must be constantly financed by issuing government bonds. The need of the United States Treasury to constantly borrow large sums has destabilized private capital markets and distorted the flow of savings into productive business activities.

The securities and investment banking industries have a long record of service to our country dating back to the early days of the Republic. As practiced in America investment banking took on a form indigenous to this country and, in a measure, has made possible the vast growth of American industry. Unlike any foreign investment banking system it has been characterized by widespread distribution facilities that have made possible the gathering and channeling of savings across the nation into the purchase of securities in a procedure known as underwriting. It is through this procedure that enterprises of all kinds, large and small, have been financed. The product of American ingenuity and inventive genius has been put to practice. Great industries have been born from rails to television, jobs have been created, and a national growth from a poor agrarian society into an unparalleled industrial giant has been achieved.

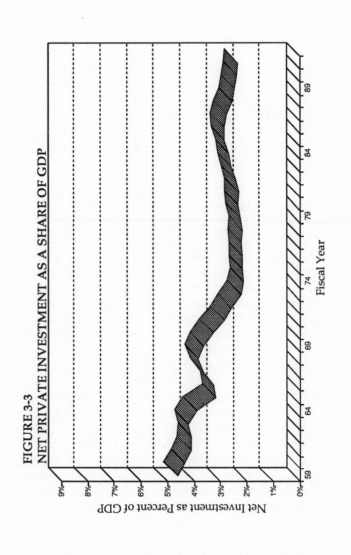

FIGURE 3-3
NET PRIVATE INVESTMENT AS A SHARE OF GDP

The ability of the capital market to channel savings into a productive industrial capacity relies upon a stable financial climate within which the value of investments can be determined. Stable capital markets encourage savers to provide the funds to create capital because the expected returns are predictably being based on such fundamental things as corporate earnings and growth. The national debt undermines financial stability by introducing elements of uncertainty about interest rates and the rate of return on alternative investments. The large overhang of national debt slows capital formation by disrupting the vital channel that allows savings to flow into productive investments.

DECLINING PRODUCTIVITY AND EARNINGS

The average American family cannot consume more if more is not produced. The nation's level of consumption is constrained by its productive capacity in the long run and thus changes in productivity determine whether the future standard of living will rise or fall. The national debt has a debilitating effect on productivity because it preempts resources that might otherwise be devoted to capital creation and technological innovation.

Productivity is measured by dividing the nation's total output by the number of hours worked by all participants in the labor force, or output-per-man-hour. Figure 3-4 compares the average annual growth rates of productivity in the United States since the 1960s. Productivity growth fell to only 0.5 percent in the 1990s, down from 2.4 percent in the 1960s. This vital sign of the nation's future economic health is ominous. And unfortunately, manufacturing productivity in the United States has grown more slowly than that of our major foreign competitors (see Figure 3-5). With the productivity growth falling behind, products made in America become increasingly expensive in relation to their overseas counterparts. Global markets and the competition from foreign producers make it impossible to pass these higher costs forward in the form of higher prices, further reducing American jobs and wages.[6]

Perhaps the most striking evidence that the national debt

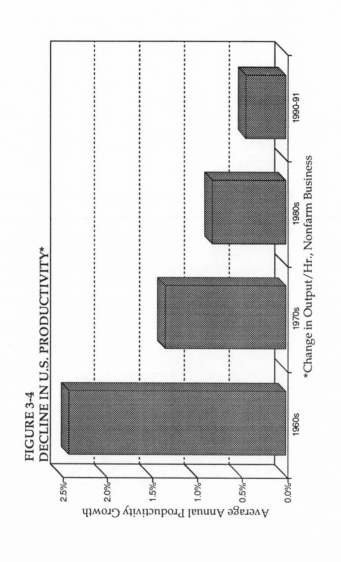

FIGURE 3-4
DECLINE IN U.S. PRODUCTIVITY*

*Change in Output/Hr., Nonfarm Business

Average Annual Productivity Growth

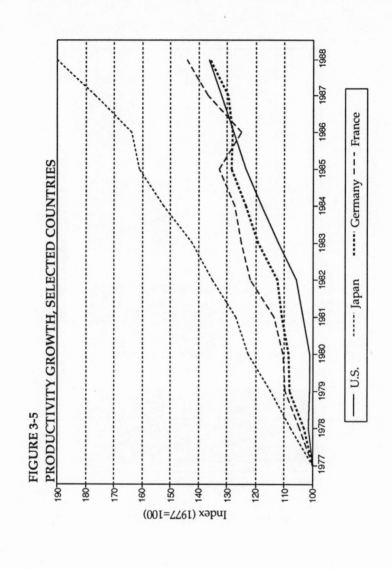

FIGURE 3-5
PRODUCTIVITY GROWTH, SELECTED COUNTRIES

Index (1977=100)

——— U.S.   ······ Japan   ······ Germany   – – – France

has taken its toll on American living standards is the long-term pattern of worker earnings. These data are presented in Figure 3-6. Sluggish productivity has to bear down eventually on paychecks and this has certainly been the case. By 1991 the weekly earnings of the average American worker had declined to levels not experienced since the 1950s.

A DOWNWARD SPIRAL: LOWER EARNINGS, LOWER SAVINGS, AD INFINITUM

The vast national debt has taken its toll on worker earnings by preempting investments, slowing the pace of capital formation and constraining productivity growth. Borrowing to finance current consumption is a temporary way to satisfy the nation's appetite but must ultimately fail as a permanent method to raise the standard of living. Indeed, borrowing to consume lowers the future standard of living because it detracts from the creation of capital required to raise productivity.

But the story gets worse: when worker earnings decline, less is saved, which results in a shrinking pie of national savings for which all borrowers, including the federal government, must compete. Americans have not been making up for the profligacy of government by saving more on their own account.

For a variety of reasons related to federal government policy private savings in the United States has been anemic and insufficient to sustain large levels of federal borrowing. Importantly, incentives created by federal tax laws and in particular the income tax system penalize savings. Ideally a growth-promoting tax system would not tax savings at all. For example a consumption tax would discourage spending and increase saving as opposed to the income tax, which discourages earnings and hence savings. A moderate improvement in the tax code would at least separately treat interest earnings on savings apart from appreciation resulting from inflation. Under the present tax regime, if 10 percent is earned on a savings account, even though 9 percent of that may have just been inflationary gains, income taxes are levied on those illusory earnings.

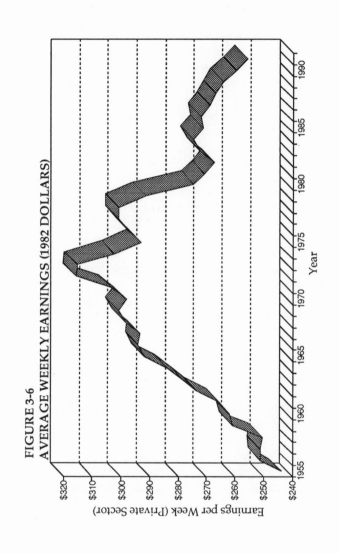

FIGURE 3-6
AVERAGE WEEKLY EARNINGS (1982 DOLLARS)

Changes in tax laws, the creation of IRAs, and financial deregulation have improved the set of government incentives toward savings, but they appear to have been too little and too late. The income tax laws work in a variety of ways to discourage business and personal savings.

LIVING ON FOREIGN SAVINGS

The pool of domestic savings in the 1980s and 1990s was too low to sustain federal deficits and at the same time maintain any significant level of borrowing by private investors to finance productive investments. The temporary "solution" was an increasing reliance on foreign savings. The influx of foreign money has only been sustained by the tenuous confidence foreign investors have in the American economy.

As more goods flowed into the United States than flowed out, paper claims to United States assets flowed out instead. For example, in 1985, Japan bought $1.9 billion in real estate in the United States, up from $0.9 billion the year before.[7] The amount of real estate bought by the Japanese tripled in 1986 to $6 billion. The Japanese experience in the United States is just emblematic of the fact that the United States became a net debtor to the tune of $107 billion in 1985. That was the first time the United States had been a net debtor since 1914. Fortunately, the United States borrowings are in denominations of its own currency. Large amounts of official reserves are held as dollars. Nearly all the debt held by foreigners is held by foreign central banks or multinational institutions. Still this process cannot go on forever. Foreigners will not keep sending goods to the United States in exchange for an ever-increasing stack of financial claims. Eventually the flow of foreign savings into the United States will begin to dry up.

The combined effects of low domestic savings and high federal borrowing are forcing the United States to rely on foreign investors to an increasingly dangerous degree. By investing in and thus acquiring ownership of the national debt, foreigners are increasing their economic power in the United States. Foreigners will be willing to lend money to

America until it can no longer make the payments. Then, as a condition for added loans, foreigner creditors will impose fiscal restrictions, territorial concessions, and so on, doing to America what America did to lesser developed nations in the 1980s and 1990s. The United States will be locked in the grasp of foreign creditors.

COMMENTARY

The national debt in the United States reached unprecedented peacetime levels by the early 1990s, a fact not ignored by financial market participants around the world. A high and growing national debt not supported by domestic private savings or the creation of productive capital places the economic future of the United States in the hands of foreign investors. Without an inflow of foreign savings the consumption spree will be self-destructive in the absence of resort to foreign wars. In which case there will be simply a postponement of self-destruction. At some point, if the continuous borrowing to pay for federal spending does not stop, the United States financial structure will collapse.

Foreign investors, who have had such untrammeled faith in the American economy, know these things as well. An abrupt flight of capital from the United States in response to the failure of the federal government to get its fiscal house in order would have grave implications for the economy. Investor concern over such capital flight underlies much of the volatility in equity markets, adding risk and instability to the process of capital formation.

Capital formation is at the heart of the long-run problem. Capital is the basis for growth. An economy cannot continue to grow if its capital stock does not grow. The national debt lowers the rate of growth of the economy by absorbing the nation's savings and preempting investments that could expand the productive capacity. This growth problem is exacerbated by the level of debt owned by foreigners because the foreign-owned debt exacerbates the United States international trade imbalance.

Economic growth normally suggests that the standard of living is rising. Unfortunately, in the 1990s the economy must grow just to service the national debt owed to domestic and foreign lenders and thus growth will be required simply to stay even. This problem will be compounded as capital formation is shoved aside by the debt and the productivity of American workers continues to fall.

NOTES

[1]In inflation adjusted dollars, personal consumption expenditures grew at an annual rate of 3.3 percent in the 1980s as compared to 3.5 percent in the 1970s.

[2]The deficit as measured against domestic savings is a more meaningful gauge of the deficit's impact on interest rates. Some analysts are of a similar accord: see Alan C. Lerner, "The Truth About the 'D' Word," *Washington Post*, April 22, 1992, p. A-21 and the survey article by Robert D. Hershey, Jr.: "Why Economists Fear the Deficit," *New York Times*, May 27, 1992, p. D-1. Because the size of the domestic savings pool is considerably smaller than national output, this gauge indicates the impact of the debt on interest rates to be far greater than comparisons to national output would suggest. In the early 1990s personal savings amounted to roughly 4 percent of GDP.

[3]The interest rate is the key determinant of the amount of resources that will be invested to create productive capital assets for two reasons. First, if a manufacturer must borrow to invest in equipment (which adds wealth through profits and creates jobs), interest rates represent an important cost of the investment. Second, if the firm already has the money, the interest rate represents an alternative use of funds. If the return on the alternative use of funds is higher than the expected return on an investment, the investment in new equipment has little appeal. For example, a high interest rate on United States Treasury securities (historically considered the most risk-free type of investment) will attract savings that might otherwise have been used for a business expansion which necessarily involves a greater risk because it would not be backed by the federal Treasury.

[4]Federal expenditures that would be defined as consumption activities include most of the entitlement programs that accounted for over half of the federal budget in the early 1990s. Programs like Social Security and Farm Price Supports are good examples of consumption expenditures that redistribute income from one group to another rather than increasing productivity.

[5]The investment portion of the federal budget comes mainly in the form of physical investment, research and development, and educational training. Spending in these areas has been falling significantly (see Figure 3-2). Not surprisingly, the public infrastructure is crumbling.

[6]Clyde V. Prestowitz, *Trading Places* (New York: Basic Books), 1989.

[7]Martin Tolchin and Susan Tolchin, "Foreign Money, United States Fears," *New York Times* Sunday Magazine (December 13, 1987), pp. 63–68.

4

Managing the National Debt

The United States of America exercises sovereign power and authority through a federal government that conducts the nation's affairs. It is a function of this government to provide services for its citizens covering a broad spectrum of needs and desires.

Throughout the years following the establishment of this government the cost of its functions had been paid for by taxes levied upon individual citizens and businesses. Generally, except in time of war, federal government revenue covered federal expenditures. During war periods the government on most occasions resorted to borrowing, but there prevailed a public determination to repay these debts, and they were repaid until the large borrowings for financing World War II were incurred. With the advent of expanding government services and their attendant costs it became expedient and politically attractive to adopt a policy of deferring repayment of past debt. New borrowing with deferral of payment made way for the painless offering of new services to the citizen. Indeed deferral of payment became truly the essence of the "free lunch" and perpetual re-election with the help of government-financed largesse. World War II debt was deferred and continues to be a portion of the national debt with repayment best classified as indefinite.

Federal borrowing was employed in the conduct of federal finances from the early days of the Republic, but the morality of credit and obligation of debt was of highest order and repayment of the federal debt was the ethical standard.[1] By reason of the policy of debt deferment and the attendant practice of manipulating maturities of the many issues of Treasury obligations that represent the national debt there can be no definite notion as to when the debt will be paid. The amorphous form in which the debt is clothed has spawned a serious misconception about the burden of the national debt. This is the fatuous proposition that because payment of the debt is deferred to the future, so also is its burden. Not so. The debt bears interest which cannot be deferred. This ever present burden permeates the fabric of every community, and its weight is increasing by the hour.

Except for expenditures made during wars, federal revenues were generally sufficient to cover the cost of government functions. However, from the period beginning in the early 1950s problems of revenue shortfalls became increasingly frequent. Revenues have been insufficient since the mid-1970s to pay even the current expense of government programs. And after 1976 the government's financial operations turned to chronic reliance upon borrowing to finance its operations. Under these circumstances surpluses were not created out of which past debts maturing during each year could be paid off, consequently the debt has not been reduced since that time. To the contrary the size of the debt has rapidly mounted. Why has this condition persisted?

Start with the premise that the federal government is spending beyond its income to provide Americans with things they want but for which they do not want to pay, or for which their political leaders will not ask them to pay. With this insight the politicized core of this vast economic problem becomes apparent and the broad span of its presence in our society more comprehensible.

The official estimate furnished by the Office of Management and Budget (OMB) for fiscal year 1992 showed federal revenue of $1,076 billion. The greater part of this would come from income and payroll taxes. Estate, gift, highway, airport, customs, and other excise taxes and miscellaneous items provide additional revenue. Expenditures of $411 billion would be made for Social Security and Medicare. This would leave, on the most conservative basis, $750 billion to cover the cost of all other expenses. First, there would be $200 billion of net interest to be paid to private investors on the $4,000 billion national debt.

There are other costs, among the largest of which were $308 billion for defense and national security, $80 billion for payment to depositors in failed savings and loans, $78 billion for federal retiree pensions, and $34 billion for veterans benefits. In addition there are the costs of the three branches of government: executive, legislative, and judicial, which would claim about $25 billion.

After payment for all these costs $25 billion remains in the till. OMB estimated that government would spend $1,441 billion of which $365 billion would be borrowed. In broad terms the federal government has borrowed to buy everything it furnishes where federal income cannot stretch.

Federal expenditures are classified on the basis of whether they are discretionary or nondiscretionary. The distinction between these two categories is becoming artificial and blurred, and this acts to facilitate the expansion of spending for virtually every kind of service that government can supply. And the clamor of citizens for more services is not subsiding. It would seem that federal borrowing will continue its course at least as long as there are funds to be borrowed.

With the federal budget in deficit, the nation only has three alternatives in dealing with its creditors: to refuse to pay (debt default); to create additional currency (debt monetization); or to pay its creditors with newly-borrowed funds (debt refunding). It should be clear that each of these options has negative consequences for a healthy, vibrant economy, with default being the most obvious case in point. The policy is deferral of debt payment. It is implemented by the practice known as refunding. In combination these most nearly constitute the debt management policy of the U.S. Treasury in the post-World War II period. As we shall see, however, debt refunding cannot go on indefinitely and at some point, unless sufficient revenues to the Treasury are forthcoming through increased taxes and other sources, or expenditures are decreased, or a combination of these, the nation will be left with only two options: debt monetization or default, either separately or together. Fears that the debt eventually will be monetized in the 1990s can stimulate inflation and hold long-term interest rates at levels higher than desirable for wholesome economic growth. And some analysts in the early 1990s advocated default as a preferable alternative to the long, painful slide that accompanies constant debt refunding, or the inflationary consequences of debt monetization.[2]

REFUNDING POLICY

The debt is not a lump-sum amount that will mature at some future date. Instead the national debt is composed of many denominations having different maturities with portions being paid at each stated maturity. It must be understood, however, that the total debt obligation of the federal government has not been extinguished or reduced in part by these payments. Simultaneously upon the payment of any maturing obligation a new obligation has been substituted.

Federal government borrowing rolls out as an endless stream of revolving debt represented by new issues of securities of varying denominations, rates of interest, and maturities. Such new issues are sold and delivered to the lenders. The proceeds of these transactions are received by the Treasury to pay off maturing federal debt or are covered into the general receipts of the Treasury for other government uses. Existing debt is being paid at maturity but only by the refunding procedure where new debt is substituted for old debt and larger debt for smaller debt. In this way growing federal deficits have been financed in a continuing process imbedded in management of the debt. Part of the existing debt is constantly being paid off, rolled over and re-issued by the Treasury. In the grip of this revolving mechanism the debt is never extinguished.

Federal government borrowing from the public is conducted mainly through a procedure of competitive bidding where the Treasury periodically offers three classes of federal securities. These are: (a) Treasury Bills ("T-Bills"), which are short-term securities of less than a year in maturity; (b) Treasury Notes, which are 1 to 10 years in maturity; and (c) Treasury Bonds, which typically have a maturity of 5 years or more. Financial instruments such as these in various denominations and maturities have been issued and continue to be sold by the Treasury to persons throughout the world. At any given time these outstanding obligations of the United States compose in the aggregate the national debt. The debt would seem to have achieved constant life through perpetual refunding. But this is subject to a condition: every instrument representing the debt mandates the payment of interest.

The refunding policy of the government has significant implications for the performance of American and international capital markets. U.S. Treasury securities have become an increasingly larger component of these markets. Figure 4-1 illustrates that federal borrowing accounted for about 40 percent of total borrowing by U.S. public and private nonfinancial institutions in 1990, up from 22 percent in 1981. A consequence of this large federal government component of the debt is that investors pay close attention to the behavior of the Treasury. When the Treasury continually ventures into the capital markets on forays to finance existing debt, it puts upward pressure on interest rates over time and creates uncertainty. Constant refunding of a massive national debt is not conducive to a stable environment for investment decisions.[3]

Serious questions arise as to whether the foreign and domestic buyers will purchase the Treasury bonds to the extent needed, and at what interest rate. This makes for an

FIGURE 4-1
FEDERAL SHARE OF TOTAL U.S. BORROWING

increasingly speculative game. When demand for the Treasury bonds is softer than expected the price falls and interest rates rise, and then stocks become a relatively less attractive investment. The opposite case can also prevail. If the demand for Treasury bonds is greater than anticipated, the price will rise, interest rates fall and stocks become more in demand. Even credit for the U.S. Treasury is finite, and the outcome of these Treasury auctions becomes less predictable as the size of the debt that must be financed and refinanced increases.

THE GROWTH OF INTEREST PAYMENTS

The level of interest payments on the public debt, as with the enormous size of the debt connection, the deficit itself, is without historical precedent in the United States. It is these interest payments that threaten the financial stability of the country. In the 1960s, interest on the federal debt averaged $12.8 billion a year (see Figure 4-2). Interest payments in the early 1980s averaged $134.6 billion a year, over ten times the level in the 1960s.

It is informative to compare interest payments on the debt to national income. Such comparisons provide a sense of the ability of the economy to service interest costs. Aside from an interlude during the Civil War, interest as a percent of gross national product (GNP) was relatively modest until the 1920s.[4] Interest was only 0.8 percent of GNP after the War of 1812 and 2.6 percent after the Civil War. Interest payments on public debt as a percent of GNP soared during World War I when the ratio rose to 2.8 percent.[5] After World War II, the interest-to-GNP-ratio fell to 1.34 percent in 1955 in concert with historically low interest rates prompted as an objective of the Treasury and Federal Reserve Board. To keep interest rates low the Federal Reserve Board turned on the monetary spigots and inflated the economy. For the two decades from 1970 to 1990, interest payments on the debt more than doubled as a share of GNP, rising to about 3.6 percent from 1.58 percent. Net interest on the national debt reached $196.3 billion in 1991 as compared with only $14 billion in 1970.

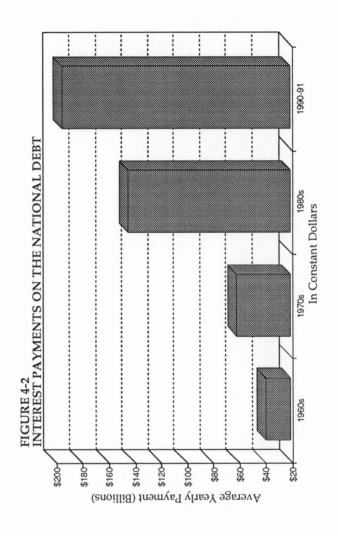

FIGURE 4-2
INTEREST PAYMENTS ON THE NATIONAL DEBT

Average Yearly Payment (Billions)

$200
$180
$160
$140
$120
$100
$80
$60
$40
$20

1960s   1970s   1980s   1990-91

In Constant Dollars

Interest Payments and the Federal Budget

These large interest payments swamp feeble attempts at deficit reductions. The problem is that a moderate increase in the deficit as a percentage of GNP can lead to massive increases in debt servicing costs. A $200 billion deficit adds nearly $20 billion in interest payments. Consider the case if Congress, overtaken with fiscal resolve, decided to cut $20 billion out of the budget. (A $20 billion a year cut is equivalent to tossing out a medium-sized cabinet department, such as the Department of Labor.) While certainly a step in the right direction, a reduction of even this amount would be grossly inadequate; the savings is wiped out by interest payments. Interest payments are a "fiscal black hole" that do not foster desirable national objectives. Yet the government pays in debt service more than half of what is spent on national defense and more than is spent on helping the poor.

The story though does not end here. As Chapter 3 made clear, the use of savings to service the debt deprives businesses of vitally needed resources that are required to create jobs and to make workers more productive.

ALTERNATIVES

The government could default on interest payments. This is not without precedent. Twentieth century revolutionaries, in moments of grandeur, have swept away the public debt with the stroke of a pen, however, foreign creditors were not amused. Closer to home, several states in the United States defaulted in the 1930s, particularly on bonds to finance canal construction. A number of Third World and Eastern European countries have effectively defaulted, although Western bankers have avoided admitting this for fear of the impact on their balance sheets. To join the grand ranks of the basket-case economies of Eastern Europe and the Southern hemisphere would not do much for the credit rating of the American government. Heretofore, federal securities have been considered the least risky of assets. Default would catapult financial markets into chaos and massive economic paroxysm.

Default is another kind of tax. The only thing certain about the debt is that someone will pay it through some form of tax. In the case of default, interest payments and the debt would have become the financial burden of the people who hold the debt, and because they would not be repaid they would end up holding the bag, as it were, something for which they did not bargain.

Inflating Our Way out of Interest Payments

Another alternative is for government to inflate its way out of burdensome interest payments. This can be done by paying for the debt by "printing" money. Abba Lerner, a British economist, was one of the first academics to propose economic policy guidelines advocating this approach. He suggested three simple targets to control economic cycles:

> First, the adjustment of total spending (by everybody in the economy, including the government) in order to eliminate both unemployment and inflation, using government spending when total spending is too low and taxation when total spending is too high; second, the adjustment of public holding of money and of government bonds, by government borrowing or debt repayment, in order to achieve the rate of interest which results in the most desirable level of investment; and third, the printing, hoarding or destruction of money as needed for carrying out the first two parts of the programs.[6]

This theory was called "Functional Finance" as opposed to the theory of "Sound Finance," which calls for balanced budgets. The Federal Reserve Board creates money by purchasing securities issued by the Treasury. The Fed is not permitted to buy newly issued interest-bearing obligations of the government, but it can purchase old bonds. The Fed then creates reserve accounts for credit at banks, and these reserves are legal tender. Banks can earn income by lending out these surplus reserves. These bank loans expand the money supply, which technically is known as "monetizing the debt".[7]

To understand this process of monetizing the debt more fully, consider what happens if the Treasury sells its securities to the public. The public exchanges money for bonds, and the Treasury spends the money. The money that comes from the public is recirculated, and there is no increase in the money supply. On the other hand, if the Fed buys the bonds and the Treasury spends the money, there is a net increase in the money supply.

Inflation is also a way to avoid raising tax rates explicitly to pay for debt services, but inflation is a tax by another name. As a prominent twentieth century economist noted,

> It is common to speak as though when a government pays its way by inflation, the people of a country avoid taxation. We have seen that this is not so. What is raised by printing notes is just as much taken from the public as is a beer-duty or an income tax. What a government spends, the public pays for. There is no such thing as an uncovered deficit.[8]

Inflation acts as a tax by devaluing the assets people hold. Inflation is simply a more elaborate and indirect means of default. Debt retirement through inflation does spread the burden of interest payments more widely but at the cost of the immense economic dislocation brought on by the inflation.

To pay off a $4 trillion government debt through printing paper money would cause an inflationary spiral rivaling that of Bolivia in the early 1980s. Bolivia's rate of inflation had then reached such levels that paper to print currency, worthless currency albeit, was the principal import. In 1986, the amount of cash, checks, and near money came to about $3.48 trillion.[9] An immediate monetizing of the debt would hence increase the money supply by 68 percent. During the 1979 inflationary episode, the money supply increased by less than 10 percent. To inflate the economy at several times that rate would cause immense uncertainty in transacting economic affairs. The economy could not adjust efficiently to such a rapid change in prices.

Interest Payments versus Monetary Policy

The reality is that the government, unless it either changes its spending habits or raises taxes, or both, must inflate its way out of interest payments if it is to avoid outright default. To continue to issue debt without financing it through money creation leads to a simple result: the economy is sent into a severe downturn. Economists Robert Solow and Alan Blinder made this point in the early 1970s in an effort to discredit the doctrine of monetarism: the idea that the supply of money alone determines the overall evolution of the economy.[10]

The fundamental monetarist policy is that a stable rate of growth of the money supply insures a stable rate of growth of the economy. Solow and Blinder argued that it might not be possible to maintain a stable rate of growth of the money supply without destabilizing the economy. Monetary policy cannot be set independently of fiscal policy in the long run. A similar argument has been made by economists Thomas Sargent and Neil Wallace. They point out that it is simply not feasible to keep running deficits without eventually increasing the money supply. The choice is not whether to monetize the debt, but whether to monetize the debt now or later. Otherwise the government would be forced to submit to insolvency.

The mathematics of the Sargent-Wallace thesis is, as always, technically complicated, but leads it to the inexorable conclusion that *interest rates* are the culprit. As an illustration, assume the economy falls into a severe slump: unemployment rises, businesses earnings decline, and tax revenues fall. If the government does not lower spending, a budget deficit will inevitably follow. Eschewing money creation, the Treasury must sell more bonds to finance this deficit. In order to attract buyers for these newly issued bonds, a higher interest rate must be offered. But as interest rates rise, future deficits are increased because the cost of debt service goes up. More bonds must, therefore, be issued to finance subsequent budget deficits. This pattern continues to feed on itself, and the national debt just piles up along the way. Where does this cycle end?

The unpleasant conclusion of the analysis is that if the interest rate, adjusted for inflation, is greater than the rate of growth of the economy, the supply of bonds required to finance federal borrowing continues to escalate. Stated differently, the growth in national income must be greater than the growth in interest payments or the economy can ill afford to expand. When the growth in interest costs outstrips the growth in interest payments, interest rates will continue to rise and the economy will deteriorate because the cost of private investments increases and the creation of capital dwindles. The moral of this analysis is that an escalating national debt, with growing interest payments, will eventually stifle productive investments and cripple economic growth.

Sound hypothetical? In the 1990s the real rate of interest on the public debt was greater than the real rate of economic growth. This has not always been the case. Before the 1980s, GDP growth exceeded the pretax real rate of interest; after 1980 the situation reversed. Beware.

COMMENTARY

Massive interest payments on the national debt are engulfing the budget and threaten America's stature as a world power. There is ample historical precedent for this. Philip II of Spain presided over one of the largest empires the world had seen. He also lorded over an irresponsible fiscal policy. His indulgence caused the Spanish government to owe more in interest to French and Italian bankers than the Spanish state was receiving in revenue. The launching of the Spanish Armada against Britain was in fact a last desperate attempt to restore the squandered glory of a state that had been decimated by extravagant borrowing and consequent interest payments. The crushing of the Armada by British frigates merely hastened the subsequent eclipse of the Spanish empire which the fiscal folly of its sovereign had preordained.

NOTES

[1]Alexander Hamilton saw this principle very clearly and went about establishing the credit worthiness of the young Republic. In 1790 he enjoined upon Congress the wisdom of assuming the Revolutionary War debt, which it could have ignored. By this act the U.S. government established its financial honor and gave rise to the expectation of future reliability.

[2]See for example the survey article by Kathleen Day, "With Debt Burgeoning, Could the U.S. Default?" *Washington Post*, June 14, 1992, p. H–1.

[3]Refunding has an additional consequence that is detrimental to economic growth. When the Treasury uses borrowed funds to pay off maturing debt obligations the money supply is reduced.

[4]Interest as a share of GNP is used for these comparisons because the historical data are reported in terms of GNP.

[5]Council of Economic Advisers, *The Economic Report of the President, 1992*, p. 395.

[6]Abba Lerner, "Functional Finance and the Federal Debt," *Social Research*, February 1943, pp. 39.

[7]In 1987, about 10 percent of the federal debt was purchased by the Fed; see Paul Courant and Edward Gramlich, *op. cit.*, p. 31.

[8]John Maynard Keynes, *A Tract on Monetary Reform* (London: The MacMillan Co.), 1923, p. 62.

[9]Council of Economic Advisers, *The Economic Report of the President, 1987*, p. 320.

[10]Alan Blinder and Robert Solow, "Does Fiscal Policy Matter?" *Journal of Public Economics*, 2 (November 1973), pp. 319–337.

5

National Debt and the Average American

Chapter 3 presented a macro perspective of the debt's toll on the earnings of the average American worker, which has resulted in the slow but sure consequence of anemic capital accumulation. Real earnings in 1991 had fallen to their lowest level since 1958, and the pattern exhibited in Figure 3-6 foreshadows an ominous trend for the remainder of this century. A shrinking ability to afford those things that American's once took for granted is hard not to notice. But connecting the dwindling living standard to the increasing national debt is complex.

Confusion about the cause of the decline in American living standards feeds the political motivation to continue federal borrowing, rather than to cut spending or raise taxes. Borrowing can be the best option from the perspective of a politician who must constantly assess the near-term electoral risks. More federal spending and deferral of payment is a surer route to reelection than cutting out programs, or increasing taxes, or some combination of the two.

The day is rapidly approaching when this political calculus will no longer be valid. When the burden from the costs of increased debt becomes excessive, borrowing is no longer politically palatable. The costs of the national debt are not an abstraction detached from the daily lives of American families. The consequences of debt deferral policy are intertwined with practically every facet of the average American's life-style. The debt functions to deprive American's of the things they most cherish: a home, an education, quality health care, retirement security, and essential services provided both publicly and privately. As incomes are eroded and the cost of living is pushed ever higher, the impact of the debt will become increasingly apparent to voters. And when this recognition occurs their elected representatives will be held accountable for failing to provide a solution for the increase of debt. The political equation will then change. The question is how far living standards will have deteriorated before voters refuse to tolerate further federal borrowing. The national debt was built upon a foundation of political motives. So too will its ultimate elimination.

The national debt is a vice that squeezes the average American from all sides: lower incomes, higher taxes to pay its carrying charges, higher prices and interest rates, and an uncertain retirement. Participation in privileges associated with a high standard of living has become tenuous.

SOMEBODY'S USING YOUR CREDIT CARD

Joseph J. DioGuardi, a certified public accountant who served in Congress from 1985 through 1988, constructs what the average taxpayer's bill would look like if it were arranged as a credit card statement. His results for fiscal year 1991 are presented in Table 5-1. DioGuardi points out that while the U.S. government never sends out such a notice, the federal budget is the one charge account that is getting the typical American most deeply into debt.

Table 5-1 illustrates that the average taxpayer paid $9,325 in federal taxes in 1991. A major portion of this payment, $1,725 or almost one-fifth, was a "finance charge" which was each taxpayer's share of the annual interest on the national debt. This $1,725 finance charge was the third largest item on the statement, ranking only below "social security and

TABLE 5-1
AVERAGE TAXPAYER'S BILL FOR FISCAL YEAR 1991*

DESCRIPTIONS	BALANCES	CHARGES	PAYMENTS
Individual Debt (Beginning 1991)	$28,796.75		
Social Security and Medicare		$3,305.34	
National Defense		2,411.63	
Income Security and Welfare		1,514.96	
Health		629.94	
Education, Training, Employment		367.07	
Agriculture, Natural Resources		297.10	
Transportation		279.04	
Administration of Justice		108.81	
Other		1,064.42	
Individual Share of Income Taxes			$4,140.05
Social Security Taxes and Contributions			3,504.52
Other			1,681.36
TOTALS		$9,978.31	$9,325.93
Finance Charge		$1,725.77	
Individual Debt (Ending 1991)	$31,174.89		

*Adapted from DioGuardi, *Unaccountable Congress, 1992*

medicare" and "national defense". The charge for each of the following categories was less than the finance charge: "income security and welfare"; "health"; "education, training, and employment"; "agriculture, natural resources"; "transportation"; and "administration of justice".

The DioGuardi accounting structure puts in vivid perspective the formidable sacrifice the average taxpayer makes because of federal borrowing. The $1,725 finance charge did not purchase any valued service or add to the nation's wealth. Its sole purpose was to cover the deferral of payment on government spending in 1991 and in prior fiscal years. At the end of fiscal year 1991 the outstanding "balance due" was $31,174, which was each taxpayer's share of the total national debt and reflects the cumulative amount of all past deferred payments. At the beginning of the 1991 fiscal year the outstanding balance due was $28,766, which means the federal government borrowed (deficit financed) an additional $2,408 per taxpayer in 1991 alone. Of course, this incremental borrowing in 1991 increased the finance charge for 1992 and will continue to add to the finance charges at a compounding rate for as long as the balance due is unpaid.

What might the average American taxpayer have purchased with an extra $1,725 in 1991? The answer of course is as diverse as the tastes of American families: from the purchase of a new personal computer, to a down payment on a car, to saving for a college education. Finance charges to carry the national debt purchase nothing of value yet deprive families of a host of goods and services they work hard to attain.

RUNNING HARDER, FALLING FURTHER BEHIND

American's real earnings are at 1950s levels in part because of declining productivity, as Chapter 3 spells out. But high rates of inflation that occurred at various intervals between 1950 and 1990 have also contributed to this decline. "Real" earnings are the nominal dollars a worker receives divided by the price level. The overall consumer price index increased 465 percent between 1950 and 1991 (see Figure 5-1), which diminished the purchasing power of nominal incomes. A car that cost $5,000 in 1950 cost $23,257 in 1991. The family that spent $50,000 on a college education in the late 1980s would have spent $10,750 in the 1950s. Prices have plainly gone through the roof. Things that were affordable 40 years earlier were out of reach for many American families in the 1990s. Why?

The connection of the debt to price inflation is threefold. First, the debt depresses productivity growth by preempting resources that would otherwise be used for investments in productive plants and equipment. Productivity lags put upward pressure on manufacturers' costs which are passed along to consumers in the form of higher prices. Second, the debt raises interest rates. A high interest rate raises the cost of consumer "durables", things such as appliances, cars, and homes, for which most Americans must borrow to purchase. Third, the debt causes inflation when it is financed by selling Treasury securities directly to the Federal Reserve. If the

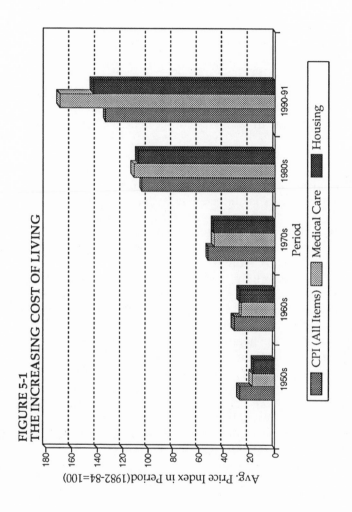

FIGURE 5-1
THE INCREASING COST OF LIVING

Avg. Price Index in Period (1982-84=100)

180
160
140
120
100
80
60
40
20
0

1950s 1960s 1970s 1980s 1990-91

Period

CPI (All Items)   Medical Care   Housing

Federal Reserve purchases U.S. Treasury securities, a practice called *seignorage*, it does so by creating (printing) money.
And as the Fed releases this new supply of money into the
economy, the dollar's value declines. A less valuable dollar
means that more dollars are needed to purchase goods and
services.

Two necessities that are in the American family's budget
are expenditures for health maintenance and for housing.
The costs for both of these necessities have been particularly
hard hit by the inflationary consequences of the debt.

Health Maintenance

Health maintenance is a basic feature of American family
life. That truth is reflected in spending on health services
which constitutes a large share of the average family's
budget. The Health Care Financing Administration expects
health care costs to reach 15 percent of national income by
the year 2000 up from 9.4 percent in 1980.[1] Health care costs
have been marching upward despite federal reforms of the
early 1980s. Indeed, as Figure 5-1 indicates, "marching" is a
totally inadequate metaphor: the Medical Care Price Index
increased more that 1,000 percent between 1950 and 1991.

Spending on health maintenance is a prime example of
how the national debt creates a vicious cycle in the economy
that is self-feeding and a progressively harder problem to
solve. Health care spending is a major component of the
federal budget and accounted for over 40 percent of the total
spent on health care in the United States in 1980s. This
federal share of health care costs has grown from about 25
percent in the 1960s. Massive federal spending on health
care has thus contributed to the annual budget deficits and
this accumulates in the national debt. One reason for the
increase in health care spending, both public and private,
has been the rapid increase in its price.

Why have health care prices risen so dramatically? The
national debt, by increasing interest rates and crowding out
private investments, has retarded productivity in the health
care sector. Slow productivity growth naturally results in
higher costs, and has been fueling much of the rise in health

spending. While federal health expenditures have risen to keep up with rising health maintenance costs, federal revenues to pay for these expenditures have not keep pace. This, of course, adds to the national debt, further slows investments and productivity, and drives health costs ever higher. The thing grows by what it feeds upon.

Housing

A majority of Americans own homes. Home ownership is what distinguishes the life-style of the typical American family from most of the world. For the average American a home is the principal means of accumulating wealth, as well as a source of important tax advantages. Housing is one of the hardest hit sectors in the U.S. economy when interest rates are pushed higher by the national debt. The "shelter" price index shown in Figure 5-1 increased by 565 percent between 1953 (the initial year for which this index was computed) and 1991.

The housing market is sensitive to interest rates for two reasons. First, the price of a home for most Americans includes a substantial interest component, represented by the mortgage. Most home mortgages are financed over long periods of time, 20 to 30 years, and interest is the biggest cost of buying a house. For example, on a $110,000 home, a homeowner having made a $10,000 down payment will pay about $215,000 in interest costs on a 30 year, 10 percent mortgage. If interest rates go up 2 percent, interest costs over the life of this loan will increase by $54,360. It is no wonder that housing purchases are thwarted by high interest rates and that the housing and construction industries are hit hard by rising interest rates.

Second, housing prices are interest-sensitive because they rise when the supply of existing housing shrinks. When residential construction is preempted by high interest rates brought about by government borrowing, the number of houses declines and prices in the housing market rise.[2]

These same considerations affect renters as well, but with relatively greater impact. Higher interest costs are in part passed on to renters in the form of higher rents. Renters, however, lack the tax advantages that partially shield home-owners from the effects of higher interest rates.

RETIREMENT INSECURITY

Most Americans will rely on two sources of income for support upon their retirement from the work force: private pension plans to which they contributed during their careers and social security. The national debt undermines the value of both.

The Pension Problem

In the early 1990s pension funds constituted over a quarter of the money invested in the stock market, and thus, a considerable amount of the wealth that secures the retire-ment of the average worker was affected by the market's performance. Financial market volatility has steadily in-creased as a direct result of the growing national debt. Here the policy of constant refunding attracts underlying un-certainties. Among them are questions about how the debt will be serviced and whether demand for Treasury securities will be sufficient to keep interest rates from rising. This lack of definition has grown in tandem with the size of the debt and is reflected in greater fluctuations of stock prices. Price fluctuations add risk and can reduce the value of investment portfolios.[3]

Pension plans are partially insured by the Pension Benefit Guarantee Corporation (PBGC), a quasi-public entity backed by the federal Treasury. If a firm defaults on its pension promises, the federal government is responsible to pick up part of the tab. But the PBGC is woefully underfunded and incapable of covering a wave of pension plan defaults. Worse still, firms that have a higher risk of default on their pension obligations do not pay any more in the way of PBGC premiums. The questionable solvency of the PBGC is itself an off-shoot of the debt problem. Debt growth increases the share of the budget that must be used to pay the interest costs, and thus fewer dollars are available to meet the remaining financial obligations of the Treasury.

Programs like the PBGC will be increasingly squeezed for funds as the size of the debt continues to expand.

Another way the national debt undermines retirement security is through its inflationary pressures. Because most private sources are not indexed for inflation, a wave of debt-fueled inflation will seriously damage people dependent on fixed income sources like pensions, IRAs, or Keogh plans for their retirement security. Inflation may also erode the value of accumulated assets of small savers. Some people and some assets do benefit from inflation. However, who gains is quite arbitrary and not closely related to productive effort or financial acumen. The additional effort of trying to avoid the negative effects of inflation on one's personal balance sheet generally leads to a net loss for everyone.[4]

The pension system upon which millions of working Americans are relying for retirement income is endangered by the debt's destablizing effects on financial markets and its effect on inflation.

The Social Security Scam

The national debt undermines the quality of life for future retirees by threatening the solvency of the social security program. Because the solvency of the social security system will inevitably depend on the number of workers contributing, a stagnant economy will not create a sufficient number of jobs to support the payments to future beneficiaries. The fewer people that work, the fewer people there are to make contributions to social security through their payroll deduction. And because the debt dampens jobs and productivity growth by constraining capital formation, the long-run viability of the social security system is jeopardized.

The solvency of the social security system will come under a severe challenge in 2010 when the nation reaches the biggest transition in its history of people from an employment status to a dependent status. With the trailing off of the demographic distribution as families have fewer children, there will be fewer people to pay for social security, less than three workers to each dependent. And this demographic bulge arrives after a period when the current cohort of old people has gotten a return on its investment in the social security system that is many times their contribution into the system. The contribution-to-benefit ratio that is projected to exist in the twenty-first century cannot be sustained. The Social Security Trust Fund's resources are modest with respect to its future liabilities. Substantial revision will be on the horizon.

Americans need stable financial instruments to nurture their wealth. The increased financial volatility brought about by the national debt at once undermines the stability of all financial markets and retirement security. This gives further emphasis to the high priority of national economic strength.

COMMENTARY

The policy of deferring and postponing payment of the national debt has had deleterious consequences. The program dedicated to a conclusion of this policy is presented in Chapter 10. Fiscal policy does make a difference, and there are things that can be done to help the financial prosperity of the average American family. As we will see in Chapters 8 and 9, most of the financial history of the United States is marked by reliable and responsible debt policies. The post-World War II period is a departure from the past in this regard. By eliminating the national debt burden, federal policy can restore a progrowth economic environment that will redound to the direct benefit of the average American.

Stable, noninflationary economic growth is primarily in the interests of the typical working American. Ballooning national debt that produces speculation in financial markets and wide swings in asset values serves the interests of very few but certainly not average working families trying to nourish their savings for reasonable income security and retirement.

The absence of political courage in tackling the debt problem follows from the lack of voter pressure to demand an end to profligate fiscal practices. And until voters act in recognition of the direct connections between their personal well-being and an overgrown national debt that is too large, the problem will not end.

NOTES

[1]"National Health Expenditures, 1986-2000," *Health Care Financing Review*, No. 8, Summer 1987, p. 24.

[2]Evidence on the relationship between interest rates and housing prices is provided in Harvey Rosen, "Housing Decisions and the U.S. Income Tax: An Econometric Analysis," *Journal of Public Economics*, 11 (February 1979), pp. 1–23.

[3]Most pension funds allow little latitude in employee input over how their retirement funds are invested. Most corporate retirement plans allow employees to switch between stock and bond funds, but usually only two or three times a year, and generally it takes a month to execute the switch. This is not enough flexibility to "play" the market or to diversify risk. The effect of increased market risk on a pension plan and worker security depends on the particular way a program is structured. Most pensions are known as *defined benefit programs:* the employer guarantees a certain payment to the employee upon his or her retirement. Another major type of pension is known as a *defined contribution plan.* Here a company and the employee each make regular contributions in some fixed proportion and no set payment upon retirement is guaranteed.

[4]A good case in point is taken up in Chapter 7, where the rise and fall of the commercial real estate, and the savings and loan industries are examined in greater detail.

6

Demise of the
Social Order

Personally, I do not feel that any amount can be
properly called a surplus as long as the nation is in
debt. I prefer to think of such an item as a reduction on our children's inherited mortgage.[1]

—President Eisenhower,
State of the Union Message,
January 7, 1960.

One of the most serious consequences of the national debt is
the burden of the debt on future generations. Elected representatives chose to impose this burden, and the electorate
has the option of eliminating those officials who buried the
nation in debt. Perhaps elected officials are delivering the
fiscal programs their constituents desire. Generations too
young to vote, however, do not have such a choice in the
political process. They cannot vote on the level of debt they
inherit; they cannot affect the level of consumption the previous generation had or the net wealth bequeathed to them.
They do not have a voice or any input, just as the current
generation had no voice on the level of debt it inherited. But
the current and future generations do have a choice of acting

to reduce or increase the creation of debt.

GENERATIONAL TRANSFER OF THE DEBT BURDEN

Chapter 2 described the accumulation of federal deficits that resulted in a national debt that reached $4 trillion in the early 1990s. In 1992 the debt was rising at an astonishing $350 billion annual clip. The federal government borrowed one out of every four dollars it spent in that year.

Per Capita Debt and Government Waste

A child born at the turn of the century faced a modest per capita debt of about $16. A child born in the year 2000 will likely enter the world with a slap on the rear and a bill for $50,000.[2] This is generational debt transfer with a vengeance. If the national debt represented borrowing to finance productive, income-generating assets, the wealth of future generations might be lifted sufficiently to cover the costs of the debt burden. Unfortunately, this is not descriptive of what the debt represents. Government waste is behind much of this debt.

The Grace Commission, a blue-ribbon panel appointed by President Reagan at the beginning of his first term in 1981, included the following summary statement in its final report:

> Grace showed us the tremendous value of saving just one dollar right now. . . . The compounding calculation is that one wasteful dollar left in the budget today will amount to a cumulative seventy-one dollars in the national debt by the year 2000. . . . We found $424.4 billion in waste and inefficiencies that could be saved over the next three years. . . . Multiply that by seventy-one dollars and you've got $10 trillion. That's what we're talking about. If Congress will get with it and stop spouting off about things it knows are not true, then we'll save $10 trillion for ourselves and our grandchildren.[3]

Future Interest Payments

In 1982 the Grace Commission Report projected a national debt of $6.2 trillion in 1995 and $13 trillion by the year 2000 unless some progress is made in restraining deficits.[4] Given the actual debt levels in the early 1990s these projections are on the low side and updated projections are made in the Epilogue. A direct consequence of the explosion in the debt is an explosion in the costs of debt service. The interest on the debt is projected to be an unprecedented burden on future generations. The Grace Commission estimated that the interest on the debt will reach $541 billion in 1995 and $1.5 trillion in the year 2000.[5]

Per capita interest payments in 1991 were about $230 a person. Assume that in the year 2000 the government finally gets the debt problem under control to the extent that interest payments are maintained at "only" the $1.5 trillion level. Assume further that population levels off at 260 million, which is the current demographic projection for the period. These assumptions imply that per capita interest payments will reach $5,770 a year. That figure is more than doubled if interest payments are divided by the expected number of taxpaying Americans. Furthermore, it should not be forgotten that the average American does not hold significant amounts of government debt, the interest on which might otherwise offset these large tax payments.

Interest Payments to Foreigners

The issue as to whether interest payments in general are a burden on future generations is taken up later. An important development, however, is that ever increasing levels of the national debt are owned by non-U.S. citizens and international institutions (see Figure 6-1). If we assume that in the year 2000 foreigners will hold about 15 percent of the debt, about the same proportion of the debt they held in the early 1990s, at the beginning of the next century the next generation will be paying around $225 billion a year in interest payments to foreigners. That means every taxpayer will be

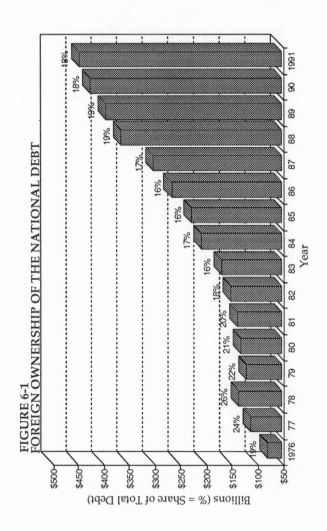

FIGURE 6-1
FOREIGN OWNERSHIP OF THE NATIONAL DEBT

writing a check for close to $850 to cover that part of the national interest charges paid to foreigners.

The process of substantial foreign participation in national debt financing began in 1973 after the first OPEC oil embargo. Middle Eastern investors, their pockets awash with surplus cash, began placing their assets in U.S. banks and federal securities. The inflow of petro-dollars was the first big bulge in foreign purchases of the public debt in the United States. With the fall of oil prices and the drying up of Saudi foreign exchange reserves, the Arab role in holding the American national debt diminished. Japan's growing wealth was propelling it toward new financial power. Japan had consistently run large trade surpluses with the United States. The purchase of U.S. assets also had been facilitated by the rise of the yen to historically high levels against the dollar, which then became cheap to the cash-rich Japanese.

The problem of foreign held debt is exacerbated by the fact that the United States is growing more in debt to foreigners than foreigners are to U.S. citizens. This export of income to foreign debt holders is also equivalent to an export of jobs. The money being paid to foreign bondholders could have been used to employ Americans. The outflow of interest income also could have been employed in raising the level of productivity in the United States. The bottom line is that the Saudis and the Japanese, among others are paid ten's of billions in debt service every year. This means that the nation is exporting future wealth in exchange for present consumption.

It should not be forgotten that in the 1980s and 1990s the nation enjoyed the benefits of previous generations' diligence. This stroke of good luck has rewarded the current generation with a stock of foreign assets. The current generation, on the other hand, is leaving future generations with a big bill payable to foreigners.

A BROADER CONCEPT OF THE BURDEN ON FUTURE GENERATIONS

The debt of the federal government does not give the full sense of the debt to be inherited by future generations. The

burden on future generations is their inherited future liabilities. State and local government debt, for example, is also
a burden on future generations. This broader conception is
often slighted in discussing the burden on future generations. Boston University Professor Lawrence Kotlikoff, a
leading expert on intergenerational effects of the federal
budget, makes the following point:

> Resources are generally scarce both at a point in
> time and over time; hence, any positive (negative)
> net transfer negative (positive) net transfers from
> younger or future generations. Economic deficits,
> as defined here, are government policies that re-
> distribute resources from younger to older gene-
> rations. This definition of economic deficits may
> seem odd to those accustomed to viewing deficits
> as the excess of "spending" over "taxes", and "defi-
> cits" are quite arbitrary and provide little basis for a
> systematic discussion of government policy.[6]

Social Security Liabilities

Social security is a major component of fiscal policy that
bears on intergenerational transfers. Unfunded social security liabilities are a tremendous burden being inherited by
future generations. The popular conception of social security
envisions a dedicated bank account held by the government
and brimming with payroll taxes. A citizen makes his FICA
payment, and the government holds part of it for him until
he retires. This popular conception is simply wrong. The
government takes the payroll tax money from working
Americans and converts it into the general receipts of the
Treasury. It is then used to pay obligations of the government, including distributions to qualified retirees. The current working generation gets a credit in the social security
accounts. Upon their retirement in the future an amount related to this credit will be paid to those current workers by
the next generation of working Americans.

This intergenerational Ponzi scheme started to flounder
when it began to encounter demographic and productivity
trends identified in the late 1970s. The entrance of women

into the labor force and cultural changes have led to a slowing of the rate of growth of the population and an older age-structure. That means the social security liability is being divided by a fewer number of children than if the population had grown at the previous rate.

As discussed in the previous chapter, the rate of productivity in the United States has also suffered from a long-term decline. Thus, the next generation will be inheriting an unprecedented burden without as many workers to support payments to retirees as required by the system.

MECHANISMS FOR TRANSFERRING THE BURDEN TO FUTURE GENERATIONS

Preempting Capital Formation and Competitiveness

One important manner in which the debt burdens future generations is by impeding capital accumulation. The next generation is poorer by the return that would have accrued to investors if they had employed their loans to increase future levels of production.

What is the nation losing when it loses a dollar's worth of investment? What is the consumption value of a lost dollar of investment? Losing a dollar of investment has a "multiplier" effect because a net contribution to future and current income is lost. Some of this contribution would have been saved, which would have further enhanced investment. If an additional dollar of investment is worth about $3 as some studies indicate, the $50 billion in lost investments in the first half of the 1980s from deficit spending, reduced the worth of future generations by $150 billion.

First rate competitive abilities have constantly been in the forefront of capitalistic societies. Competition is built into our economic structure by various market norms and legal edicts. Politicians and business people express emphatic consternation about growing market domination achieved by Japan, Germany, Korea, and others surpassing the United States in competitiveness in world markets. No one wants the next generation to inherit a backwater nation incapable of generating products of the best quality for which there will be a market, but in which America's share will be shrinking. Debts and deficits hurt national competitiveness by reducing the available resources to produce products for export as explained in Chapter 3. The loss of these exports diminishes the stock of job-specific skills in the workforce that contribute to the nation's ability to maintain and expand its position in global markets.

Tax Avoidance and Productivity

A second mechanism for shifting the national debt burden comes in the form of tax avoidance. This is similar to the effect discussed previously except that instead of eliminating investments outright, purchases are made that would not have been except for tax advantages. People invest in tax shelters, send money abroad, barter services, or simply produce less just to avoid taxes. These are things they might not have been done if taxes were low.

Table 5-1 showed that nearly one-fifth of the average taxpayer's bill goes to pay finance charges on past debt. A tax-induced distortion of the economy is another way of saying that more is lost in money and well-being from levying a tax than is gained in revenue from the tax. The higher the future taxes are levied to pay interest costs on the debt, the higher this distortion will be. Consequently higher taxes in the future implies higher distortions in the future, relative to the imposition of taxes now. This will impose a loss on future generations for which there will be no semblance of compensation.

COMMENTARY

For those who do not believe the debt is a burden on current or future generations, why not raise the debt even more? What difference would another trillion or two make if "we owe it to ourselves"?[7] It makes a big difference. The nation is consuming and investing a lot more than it is producing. This is being sustained by pledging our present and future production for loans increasingly held by foreign residents to provide for national consumption. This could go on until the cost of debt service has consumed so much of the economy that citizens will find the conditions unbearable. Revolt will follow with repudiation, and a new system will replace the present one. The debt is on its way to forcing a generational separation in our society. Future citizens may feel no legal or moral obligation to accept these burdens imposed by previous generations.

The current generation has raised its consumption by increasing the issue of government debt at the expense of the next generation's standard of living. Those lending the money have not suffered because they have been compensated with future interest payments, but the net result is a diminution of the nation's capital stock. Debt accumulation cannot be sustained if our system of capitalism and freedom is to survive. This leads to repudiation and forfeiture of the value of accumulated capital and wealth.

The post-World War II generation is perhaps the most irresponsible in the United States history. In the words of James M. Buchanan, "The fiscal outcomes of ordinary politics now resemble the behavior of the compulsive gambler who finds himself in Las Vegas or Atlantic City".[8] No other generation has so blatantly impoverished the prospects of the next-in-line on the generational ladder. There are inadequate rates of productivity growth, massive unfunded social security liabilities, a pathetic level of savings, and a beleaguered international competitiveness. The collapse of fiscal integrity during this period does not bode well for future generations.

NOTES

[1]Quoted in William G. Bowen, Richard G. Davis, and David Kopf, "The Public Debt: A Burden on Future Generations," in James Ferguson (ed.) *The Public Debt and Future Generations* (Chapel Hill, NC: University of North Carolina Press), 1964, p. 67.

[2]Grace Commission Report, 1984.

[3]*Ibid.*

[4]*Ibid.*

[5]This figure is based on the Grace Commission's projected debt in the year 2000 and the projected population of 260,378,000 for the United States provided in the U.S. Bureau of the Census, Current Population Reports, Series P-20, No. 363, *Population Profile of the United States, 1980* (Washington, DC: U.S. Government Printing Office), 1981.

[6]Lawrence Kotlikoff, "Economic Impact of Deficit Finance," *IMF Staff Papers*, Vol. 31, September 1984, p. 553.

[7]President Franklin D. Roosevelt used this expression in the 1930s when he advocated deficit financing to fund programs in the New Deal.

[8]James M. Buchanan, "Public Debt and Capital Formation" in Dwight Lee (ed.), *Taxation and the Deficit Economy* (San Francisco: Pacific Research Institute for Public Policy), 1986, pp. 177–194.

7

Profligate Spending and Revolving Error: Carter to Reagan to Bush

Presidential politics requires a domestic economic agenda. The campaign trails of America are littered every 4 years with platforms to eliminate wasteful spending, reduce taxes, cut the deficit, deregulate enterprise, boost productivity, bring down inflation, rebuild the nation's infrastructure, and whatever else may have some political advantage at the time. Position papers and speeches promulgate visions of prosperity and occasionally a view of how those with a penchant to be president would lead us onward to the promised land. Someone puts together a coalition, gets elected, and then there are miles of pledges to keep. But promises to reduce the national debt have not been kept as even powerful administrations become powerless to arrest the mounting acceleration of the national debt.

Some post-World War II presidents championed the use of deficit-financed spending programs and made no apologies for the unbalanced budgets presented in the cause of offsetting recessionary phases of the business cycle. The spending programs of Presidents Kennedy and Johnson immediately come to mind. But this ideological belief that deficits are ultimately helpful was not embraced by Presidents Carter, Reagan, and Bush. Here were three presidents, each of whom ran successfully on platforms opposed to big government and further proliferation of government programs. They were committed to balancing the federal budget. Yet none were able to make this happen. During these three administrations Democrats and Republicans alike were in the White House and each party took a turn controlling at least one branch of Congress. All three administrations witnessed a period that did not, at least by historical standards, demand an extensive or costly engagement of the U.S. Armed Forces.[1] But the national debt rose to levels that had previously been seen only during wartime, and each succeeding administration saw the debt at a greater size.

The presidential baton that passed from Carter to Reagan to Bush over a span of 16 years was marked by the economy's losing effort to keep pace with a rapidly expanding national debt. In fact, the debt ran far ahead. Gross domestic product (GDP) grew by 117 percent while the national debt grew by 181 percent, a difference of 63 percentage points. The average growth rate in the debt was 11.3 percent (continuously compounded) for these sixteen budget cycles, which exceeded by four percentage points the 7.4 percent average growth in the nation's GDP. This nearly tripling of the debt was fueled by the federal spending juggernaut that grew 8.1 percent per year, again faster than the economy, during the consecutive terms of these three conservative presidents.

The endeavor of these administrations, as measured by any reduction in the size or the rate of growth in the debt, is best characterized as total failure. Nor could it have been otherwise under our present politicized fiscal system. Reducing the national debt imposes pain in the short run while the rewards for eliminating the debt are not felt for a long time. What the Carter-to-Reagan-to-Bush period reveals so starkly is that the requirements for a vibrant economic process are incompatible with incentives engrafted onto the political process, and new institutions are necessary to reconcile the two. America's fiscal order cannot be restored without significant structural changes.

The tension between good politics and good economics saws away at the foundations of the social order as votes are purchased with the public purse. The strategic use of fiscal and economic policy as devices for political control is at variance with the conditions needed for fostering long-term economic prosperity. Growing economies require a stable financial atmosphere that both encourages saving and efficiently channels this nutrient into an expansion of productive capacity. The market processes to transform savings into investments and then into greater production and higher living standards need time for consummation. Yet these long-term requisites for economic strength are subordinated by the political process to the needs of short-term electoral strategies. The Carter-to-Reagan-to-Bush period in American politics (1977 to 1993) provides a considerable amount of evidence that intentions to tame big government and reinvigorate the domestic economy as proclaimed in their successful campaigns have not on either front found achievement.

THE CARTER LEGACY

The Carter campaign message is all but lost in the facts of his administration, since these bear small resemblance to his preelection rhetoric. Candidate Carter proposed to combine social liberalism with fiscal conservatism, a combination that was recycled as a "new idea" in the 1990s. Carter's platform advocated deregulation in transportation, zero-based budgeting, and a 10 percent growth in military spending, all the while cutting jobs programs and reducing social security benefits. Most of Carter's original intentions became confounded by inflation, recession, and his inability to lead the country.

Over the 4 Carter years federal spending exploded and grew by 50 percent from the time he came into office until he left: Spending went from $409 billion in fiscal year 1977 to $678 billion in fiscal year 1981 (see Figure 7-1 and Table 7-1). Federal outlays expanded at an annual rate of 12.6 percent, which was nearly two percent faster than the growth rate in

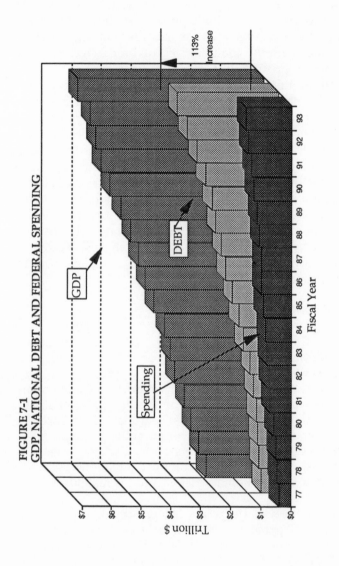

FIGURE 7-1
GDP, NATIONAL DEBT AND FEDERAL SPENDING

TABLE 7-1
GDP, NATIONAL DEBT AND MAJOR BUDGET COMPONENTS FISCAL YEARS: 1977-1993 (in Billions)*

Fiscal Year	GDP	DEBT	Total Spending	Interest Payments	Domestic Spending	Entitlement Spending	Social Security	Farm Price Supports
77	$1,922.2	$549.1	$409.2	$29.9	$197.0	$206.6	$83.7	$3.8
Carter Budgets								
78	$2,160.0	$607.1	$458.7	$35.5	$218.7	$228.4	$92.4	$5.7
79	$2,425.7	$639.8	$503.5	$42.6	$240.0	$248.2	$102.6	$3.6
80	$2,638.3	$709.3	$590.9	$52.5	$276.5	$291.5	$117.1	$2.8
81	$2,966.8	$784.8	$678.2	$68.8	$308.1	$340.6	$137.9	$4.0
Reagan Budgets								
82	$3,120.2	$919.2	$745.8	$85.0	$326.2	$372.7	$153.9	$11.7
83	$3,318.2	$1,131.0	$808.4	$89.8	$353.5	$411.6	$168.5	$18.9
84	$3,702.8	$1,300.0	$851.8	$111.1	$379.6	$406.3	$176.1	$7.3
85	$3,968.1	$1,499.4	$946.4	$129.5	$416.2	$450.0	$186.4	$17.7
86	$4,225.5	$1,736.2	$990.3	$136.0	$439.0	$459.7	$196.5	$25.8
87	$4,448.4	$1,888.1	$1,003.9	$138.7	$444.9	$470.2	$205.1	$22.4
88	$4,809.5	$2,050.3	$1,064.1	$151.8	$465.0	$494.2	$216.8	$12.2
89	$5,159.9	$2,190.3	$1,144.2	$169.2	$489.6	$527.2	$230.4	$10.6
Bush Budgets								
90	$5,456.6	$2,410.4	$1,251.8	$183.8	$501.7	$566.5	$246.5	$6.5
91	$5,638.0	$2,687.2	$1,323.0	$196.3	$532.2	$635.9	$266.7	$10.1
92	$5,830.7	$3,033.0	$1,454.0	$201.0	$547.0	$708.0	$285.0	$10.4
93	$6,238.1	$3,360.0	$1,505.0	$213.0	$538.0	$752.0	$301.0	$12.0

* Note: Federal Fiscal Years begin in October, preceding the calendar year by three months. For example, Carter took office in 1977, but his first budget for Fiscal Year 1978 did not take effect until October 1977.

GDP (see Figure 7-2 and Table 7-2). The fastest growing item in the budget was interest on the debt, which increased at an annual rate of 20.8 percent. The spending growth rate to expand entitlement programs such as social security was 12.5 percent, which were the very programs candidate Carter pledged to curtail. The growth rate in spending on domestic discretionary programs was not far behind, experiencing a 11.2 percent annual growth rate.

It is remarkable that the spending increases for virtually all major government programs was coincident with enactment of the 1974 Congressional Budget and Impoundment Act. The 1974 Act was reputed at the time to be the most radical reform of the federal budget process ever undertaken. Its many provisions sought to address the inadequate time to complete work on the budget, the Congressional inability to set spending priorities and economic policy, the lack of objective data, and the absence of spending discipline. The measure did not discipline spending, to put it mildly, nor has it fulfilled its promise to strengthen the federal budget process.

Carter's Response to the Debt

The national debt increased 36 percent during the Carter administration, or 8.9 percent on an annual basis (see Figure 7-3). The Carter record on the debt is distinguishable from that of Reagan and Bush in that not only was the growth rate of the debt slightly slower, it was actually less than the growth in GDP, which averaged 11 percent per year. Under Carter, the debt as a share of GDP shrank, a condition that did not obtain during the Reagan and Bush years that followed. And the reason the debt grew at a slower rate under Carter than under Reagan and Bush is clear: inflation. Wages and prices increased at an average yearly rate of 13 percent during the Carter presidency, as compared to 5 percent under Reagan and 4 percent under Bush. This high inflation rate mitigated the growth rate in the debt because revenues were increased by more than they would have been under a regime of stable prices. However, there was no free lunch: the Carter program of slowing debt growth by

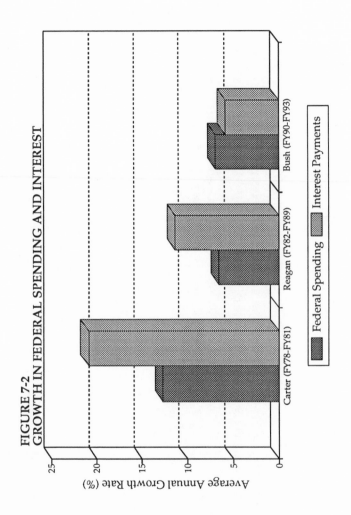

FIGURE 7-2
GROWTH IN FEDERAL SPENDING AND INTEREST

TABLE 7-2
GDP, NATIONAL DEBT AND MAJOR BUDGET COMPONENTS
ANNUAL GROWTH RATES BY ADMINISTRATION: FISCAL YEARS 1978-93

	GDP	National Debt	Total Spending	Interest Payments	Domestic Spending	Entitlement Spending	Social Security	Farm Price Supports
All (FY78-FY93)	7.4%	11.3%	8.1%	12.3%	6.3%	8.1%	8.0%	7.2%
Carter (FY78-FY81)	10.9%	8.9%	12.6%	20.8%	11.2%	12.5%	12.5%	1.3%
Reagan (FY82-FY89)	6.9%	12.8%	6.5%	11.2%	5.8%	5.5%	6.4%	12.2%
Bush (FY90-FY93)	4.7%	10.7%	6.9%	5.8%	2.4%	8.9%	6.7%	3.1%

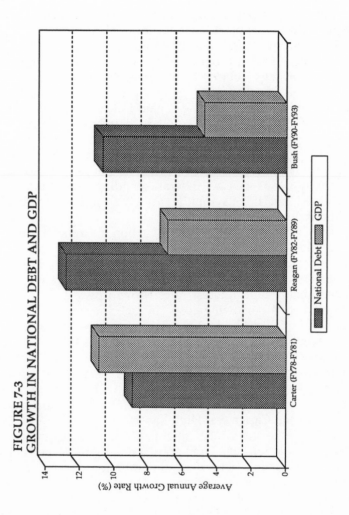

FIGURE 7-3
GROWTH IN NATIONAL DEBT AND GDP

inflation is a textbook example of how the inflation method leads to economic disorder.

Inflation caused tax revenues to increase in the Carter years without explicit changes in the tax code because federal income taxes were progressive and not indexed to the inflation rate. A progressive tax system operates to make higher earnings subject to a higher tax rate than lower earnings. And when earnings go up because of inflation, a higher proportion of income is paid in taxes even though in terms of inflation-adjusted dollars, purchasing power has not changed. This effect is commonly known as *bracket creep*. The 13 percent annual inflation rate under Carter caused federal revenues to increase faster than household earnings, if not quite as fast as federal spending. Thus the debt increased but not as rapidly as it might have increased without double-digit inflation.

The Carter program of debt reduction via inflation carried other detrimental consequences. Nominal interest rates rose sharply to compensate lenders for the expected future decreases in the value of the dollar. Naturally these exceptionally high interest rates drove upward the federal government's borrowing costs. In fact, the interest component of the federal budget grew at an average annual rate of 21 percent during Carter's 4 year tenure (see Table 7-1). The Carter debt was financed by Treasury bonds paying double-digit interest rates, the highest in the post-World War II period. Taxpayers in the year 2010 will make the final interest payment to service the 30-year Treasury bonds issued in the Carter era. High and rising interest rates also stifled private investment and national income grew less than the inflation rate. GDP grew annually by 11 percent, 2 percentage points less than the inflation rate. The real income of American workers shrank as a direct result of fiscal profligacy during the Carter administration.

An important aspect of the Carter legacy is that when the prevailing high inflation became perceived by Americans as a predictable way of life it provided the motivation to resort to real estate investing as an assured road to wealth. This together with an expectation of meeting repayment with debased dollars and exceedingly favorable tax treatment exaggerated the base that pumped up real estate prices beyond their value. Bank financing, broadly based upon extravagant expectations, had become a major participant in this development. The Revenue Act of 1986 eliminated many of these tax advantages and that punctured the bubble. And when President George Bush moved into the White House he was greeted by the bank and savings and loan crisis, a decline in construction activity, and an oncoming recession.

In short, the double-digit inflation rate increased federal revenues and made it possible for spending to expand rapidly under President Carter, without causing the national debt to grow by more than GDP. As a by-product of this approach to fiscal management, American's experienced a declining standard of living and severely distorted capital markets. And a fiscally conservative Democrat president working with a Democrat-controlled Congress armed with a newly enacted Budget Act could not reign in the debt, even with a double-digit inflation rate.

At the close of the Carter administration's single term the national debt was $784 billion, a 36 percent increase since it took control of the White House in 1977.

REAGAN'S CHALLENGE: AN ECONOMIC DUNKIRK

Ronald Reagan was elected president in 1980 with the country in a period of national "malaise" and economic distress. Reagan had appointed David Stockman as director of the U.S. Office of Management and Budget. He declared that the nation had arrived at an "economic Dunkirk". The Reagan administration thereupon launched "A Program for Economic Recovery." Michael Evans, an economist sympathetic to the Reagan-Stockman economic goals, described the program as follows:

> The Reagan program, as it was structured, asked the economy to perform not one but three unnatural acts. The first was for the gross national product (GNP) to grow faster at the same time that

the money supply growth was being severely restricted. The second was for the rate of real growth to increase from 1 percent to 5 percent at the same time that the rate of inflation was cut in half, from 10 percent to 5 percent. The third was to balance the budget by 1984 in spite of massive increases in defense spending and unprecendented tax cuts.[2]

The Reagan administration was grounded in supply-side economics. Supply-side economics is worth considering because in the presence of its practice the national debt became the largest in world history and a by-product of ostensibly conservative doctrine. It is true that supply-side economics has at times been misunderstood and maligned. While some register it a failure and others claim it to be a success, it could be argued that supply-side economics has yet to be completely tested. Having more than one side, its interpretation seems to escape a constant, and therefore dependable, evaluation.

A common reading of supply-side economics is that of George Gilder, whose book, *Wealth and Poverty*, was widely circulated in the Reagan White House. *Wealth and Poverty* was essentially a free market critique of the modern welfare state. The idea is simple: excessive growth of the government stifles economic performance and a reduction of the growth of the government, which will have supply-side effects. As a reference point contrast the supply-side vision to textbook Keynesian economics. There a device called the "balanced budget multiplier" is used to argue that an increase in government spending would stimulate growth in the economy. In the Keynesian paradigm expanding government outlays propel economic growth. The supply-side argument claims the opposite: a balanced decrease in spending and taxes is expansionary. Whatever the conceptual merits of the supply-side doctrine may be, the Reagan administration did not bring this view to the test because government spending expanded rather than contracted during Reagan's two terms from 1981 to 1988.

Federal outlays increased during Reagan's tenure at an

average annual rate of 6.5 percent, about half the rate of increase under Carter (see Figure 7-2 and Table 7-2). This difference is grossly deceptive. The Reagan campaign pledge to reign-in inflation was indeed carried out through actions taken by the Federal Reserve Bank under the leadership of its newly-appointed chairman, Paul Volker. The average inflation rate during Reagan's tenure was 4.6 percent, roughly one-third the rate under Carter. Thus, in terms of real, or inflation-adjusted dollars the federal budget grew considerably faster under Reagan than under Carter: by about 2 percent annually under Reagan as compared with 0.1 percent under Carter.

The growth in federal programs under Reagan was not limited to the widely acclaimed defense build-up. Domestic discretionary spending grew annually by 5.8 percent, which was slightly faster than the 5.5 percent growth in entitlement programs. Social security spending grew by 6.4 percent and farm price supports, another entitlement program, sprouted at an annual rate of 12.2 percent under Reagan. By comparison, farm price supports during Carter's tenure increased by 1.3 percent annually. The interest component of the budget grew by 11.2 percent annually under Reagan, which was roughly twice the growth rate in outlays generally, and, in inflation-adjusted dollars, was very close to the average increase during the Carter presidency.

Reagan Tax Reforms: Missed Opportunities for Structural Change

The double-digit inflation in the late 1970s not only pushed up interest rates, it also pushed up tax revenues through the bracket creep effect that was described earlier. If the federal tax code that existed under Carter had remained intact, some analysts project that taxes would have increased from 21 percent of GDP in 1981 to 24 percent of GNP in 1984. With inflation moving taxpayers into ever higher tax brackets, the marginal tax rate on the average worker would have reached 60 percent by 1990.[3] There was good cause to be concerned about the course of high taxes.

The big test, "riverboat gamble" as termed by the then Senate Majority Leader Howard Baker, came in 1981 with the Economic Recovery Tax Act (ERTA), a revolutionary tax reform that was clearly influenced by supply-side doctrine. ERTA lowered the top tax rate on nonservice income to 50 percent and generally cut tax rates across the board: estate taxation was relaxed; indexation of the tax system was phased in; and the tax consequences of leasing were liberalized. Perhaps the most significant measure of the Act was the introduction of the Accelerated Cost Recovery System (ACRS), which supplied more generous depreciation allowances for business.

The ERTA tax code revisions went into effect in 1982 with the notable exception of the indexation provision that would begin to be phased in 1983. This was an indication of a groping endeavor to find a stimulus to a sluggish economy. The impact of ERTA, and indeed the efficacy of supply-side theory, is difficult to assess from the events that followed. Critics of the policy are quick to point out that federal revenues did not increase as the supply-side gurus had advertised. In fact revenues were much less than anticipated, which provided empirical ammunition to refute the basic supply-side argument. But two economic conditions changed radically in 1982, and these can explain the revenue shortfall as plausibly as the failure of tax reductions to expand the economy: A cyclical recession and tight monetary policy.

With an economic recession that reduced earnings and a tight monetary policy that abruptly brought down inflation, tax revenues fell to 19.8 percent of GDP as compared with 20.2 percent the previous year. (Revenue estimates had counted on inflation to push taxable incomes into higher tax brackets because the indexation provision of the Act had not yet become effective.) With the deficit far worse than expected and a backlash against Reaganomics during the 1982 recession, there was an incentive for further groping through the field of tax legislation. In 1982 new tax legislation was enacted that aborted the transition to lower capital costs for corporations and eliminated other tax deductions passed only a year before.

The consequences of the 1981 and 1992 tax legislation go beyond the revenue deficiency and consequent additional national debt. It disrupted the nation's capital markets and the transformation of saving into productive manufacturing capacity by artificially making other investments more profitable. Tax loopholes and the expanded depreciation provisions made investments related to commercial real estate particularly profitable. Investors were eager to speculate on office buildings while the banks and savings and loans were equally eager to help. Tax shelter syndication mushroomed, and commercial space flourished. The total stock of commercial buildings in the United States doubled during the 1980s despite a huge increase in vacancy rates. The expansion of real estate lending infused an extra $300 billion of credit into the economy from 1982 to 1988.[4]

The tax law changes in 1981 along with the continuing expectations from the Carter era that real estate investments were the road to wealth under high inflation caused the balance sheet of the private sector to move deeply into debt when the value of real estate assets finally collapsed. Perhaps an even more debilitating effect of the 1981 Tax Act is that vast resources attracted to the financing of office buildings and hotels came at the expense of investing for the purpose of improving productivity and an internationally competitive manufacturing sector.

The long-term effects of the 1981 Tax Act were apparent by the end of the decade. The portfolios of banks, and especially savings and loans, were loaded to the hilt with construction loans, an industry made "profitable" largely by the tax preferences already noted. However, the tax laws were subsequently changed in 1986, which dried-up further loans to the construction industry and dealt a devastating blow to that industry and financial institutions that had previously financed construction loans. This contributed to the subsequent financial debacle in which the savings and loan industry collapsed, banks were put in jeopardy and the solvency of the Federal Deposit Insurance Corporation was threatened. The cost to the federal government from salvaging the savings of countless depositors in failed savings and loans and banks, was estimated to be as high as $500 billion. The absence of a capital market free from tax code distortions and incentives to channel resources into productive investments stalled economic growth.

Part of the rationale for the Reagan tax cuts in 1981 should not be overlooked. It was a strategy used to reduce government spending in subsequent years. By reducing revenues through a tax cut, even if it contributed further to the budget deficit, pressure would be brought to constrain federal spending. The idea was simply to starve government spending and force sound fiscal policy into practice. This strategy turned out to be ill-suited to the purpose. Government spending continued to grow at a pace far outstripping revenue growth, which of course only added to the national debt.

The federal tax code was revisited during Reagan's second term with the Tax Reform Act of 1986. This legislation contained provisions even more extreme than those enacted in 1981 and subsequently repealed. Marginal tax rates were set to descend to 28 percent, an unthinkable level two decades earlier when tax rates were 70 percent. In exchange for the lower marginal rates, a number of tax preferences were eliminated, including those that made real estate investments artificially profitable. Some features of this Act were designed to improve the efficiency of the allocation of capital. But incongruously the 1986 reform also imposed a severe burden on corporations by eliminating the lower rate that previously had been applied to taxes on capital gains. More importantly, the 1986 bill did nothing to reduce the debt (except for the temporary revenue increases in 1986 and 1987 from capital gains taxes as investors sold assets to avoid the increase in capital gains taxes scheduled to go into effect in 1988).

The reforms in 1986 like the reforms in 1981 represent a failure in that a propitious opportunity was missed to make *structural* changes in the federal tax system. In this sense, a rare opportunity escaped realization. The political climate during the Reagan years was right to eliminate the income tax all together and replace it with a savings-oriented tax system. A system that taxes consumption rather than income and profitability would have removed the disincentive effects on efficiency and productive initiative.

Such a structural change also would have resolved the issue of lowering the capital gains tax — there would be no capital gains tax to reduce. An elimination of the income tax and a substitution of a consumption tax would have set the country on a progrowth course, embracing rewards and encouragement for productivity and the benefits of necessary capital formation. With such a change productivity would necessarily have increased.

But What about the Reagan Economic Boom?

Rising real incomes in the Reagan era was the basis of much of the popularity of his presidency. Driven largely by a wave of mergers and acquisitions, the stock market flourished and the perception of the 1980s is one of a *belle epoque* of growth and reinvigoration of the American economy. Despite all of this the national debt became a greater, not a lesser problem.

The Reagan boom is perhaps exaggerated. The rapid GDP growth of 6.4 percent in 1984 following the 1981-1982 recession slipped quickly and the average real growth rate was 2.3 percent over Reagan's 8 years in office. By comparison, real annual growth rates were 4 percent in the 1960s and 3 percent in the 1970s.[5] Remarkable as this may sound, 10.6 million jobs were created during the Carter administration while only 7.8 million jobs were created during the Reagan administration.[6] Capacity utilization was weak and real wages remained below 1963 levels.[7] Two-worker families grew in order to maintain living standards. What is worse is that the deficit-fed boom was not based on domestic investment and technological progress, but instead was fueled by excess government spending for non-productive purposes and the inflow of capital from abroad. Domestic savings slumped despite the generous incentives for savings provided by supply-side tax cuts.

The Reagan Response to the Debt Crisis

The Reagan administration inherited a national debt of

$784 billion, the amount that had accumulated by the end of Carter's last budget cycle in fiscal year 1981 (see Table 7-1). The causes of the debt crises during the 8 years that followed are varied but what is equally important is the flat failure of a rock-ribbed conservative Administration to reduce the growth rate of the debt. The Republicans held majority control in the Senate and held a postwar record number of House seats. With the executive and legislative power in the same party, the political stage was apparently set for an economic agenda that would wrestle the budget back into balance and at least make progress towards debt reduction. The debt continued to grow in part because tax revenues in the 1982 fiscal year (following the 1981 tax reforms) were far less than anticipated when the original expenditure decisions were made. The revenue shortfall had several sources, among them was the failure of previous administrations to pursue policies for increasing savings and capital formation and industrial productivity. What is less easily blamed on the actions of previous administrations is the continued increase in federal spending during the Reagan years. Federal spending was not reduced in any major budget category and the Federal tax code was not reformed in a significant way to encourage long-term economic vitality. For both reasons the deficits persisted and propelled the national debt ever upward.

The Reagan administration did not use a Carter-like "inflation method" for holding down growth in the national debt. As discussed, the inflation rate was substantially curtailed by the Fed soon after the Volker appointment in 1978. Response to the debt crisis that was mounting proved to be totally ineffective. In an attempt to reduce budget deficits, Gramm-Rudman-Hollings (GRH) was passed with a goal of lowering federal deficits in yearly increments over 5 years. In its original version GRH proposed to eliminate deficits by fiscal year 1991. GRH targeted a budget deficit of $108 billion for 1988, and proposed automatic budget cuts be implemented by the Office of Management and Budget when deficit limits were exceeded. The legislation ran into Constitutional objection and was revised in several ways, including the target date at which the federal deficit would be zero.

Another tactic of the Reagan administration in handling the budget crisis was to securitize the loan portfolio held by the federal government. Securitizing loans is a common practice in the private sector. It involves packaging loans together and selling them at a deep discount to investors. The federal pilot program raised $5 billion for the government in this fashion. Privatization of the Federal loan portfolio was a sound financial move likely to improve efficiency and save costs over time. It provided only a one-time infusion of revenues, however, and cannot be expected to lower the national debt over the long run. Indeed, some analysts have argued that the revenues from federal asset sales, like tax revenues generally, were simply used to increase spending rather than to reduce the debt.

With all the campaign promises and genuine intent to harness big government, federal outlays rose by over 50 percent during the 8 years of the Reagan administration and the national debt more than doubled. The crucial lesson is that structural changes in the fiscal machinery are required to accomplish budget balance. The Gramm-Rudman-Hollings budget reforms represent an attempt to implement structural change that ultimately failed because the enforcement provisions were inadequate. Under pressure to make the required spending cuts or to raise additional revenues, Congress and the Reagan administration compromised by postponing the day of reckoning further and further into the future. The enforcement provisions and deadlines contained in GRH were easily amended and therefore ineffective constraints.

The Reagan administration expressed concerns about getting the national debt under control but was unable to unravel the fiscal puzzle that stood in its way. The average increase in the debt was 12.8 percent in each Reagan-signed federal budget, more than doubling the national debt during his presidency. And while GDP did grow modestly faster than inflation under Reagan, a definite improvement over the Carter era, the race to keep up with this growing debt was lost. America's national debt grew almost twice as fast as its output on Reagan's watch.

At the close of the Reagan administration the national debt had reached to $2.2 trillion, a 103 percent increase since its stewardship was commenced in 1981.

FEDERAL BUDGETS AND THE DEBT UNDER BUSH

Vice-president and presidential candidate George Bush had a vision in 1988: a kinder, gentler nation with a balanced budget and no new taxes. At least two components of his vision were shear fantasy. Along with his first budget submitted to Congress, for fiscal year 1990, Bush Budget Director Richard Darman unveiled a tax and spending plan he said would balance the budget by the 1993 fiscal year. The deficit in 1993 turned out to be nearly $400 billion. The Bush administration needed a better plan.

Once again, despite the campaign promises and all the good intentions to cut the size of the government, the rate of growth in federal spending actually increased to 6.9 percent annually after President Bush took his seat in the Oval office (see Table 7-2). The growth rate in entitlement spending escalated substantially to 8.9 percent per year as compared to 5.5 percent under Reagan. The growth rate in domestic discretionary spending dropped to 2.4 percent from 5.8 percent under Reagan, and the growth in interest payments on the debt fell to 5.8 percent compared to 11.2 percent under Reagan. Federal spending in the form of payments to the Federal Deposit Insurance Fund (FDIC) added roughly $65 billion annually during Bush's term, a considerable increase over the Carter and Reagan years. Under Carter's administration, and for much of Reagan's term, the deposit insurance fund added revenues to the federal budget because premiums paid by members of the FDIC generally exceeded the costs incurred by the deposit insurance fund. But in 1986 the number of failed thrifts that were involved in excessive real estate loans escalated, and the insurance fund was no longer self-sufficient. Federal payments to cover the deposit insurance shortfall rose from $1.5 billion in fiscal year 1986 to $58.1 billion in Bush's first budget in fiscal year 1990 (see Table 7-1). While this additional budgetary burden for the FDIC was substantial, it amounted to less than 15 percent of the annual budget deficits during the Bush administration.

With these rapid growth rates in federal spending the nation continued its descent into debt. Bush rejected a tax increase sufficient to cover the annual spending increase of 6.9 percent, which meant the only other alternative was more borrowing. The debt increased at 10.7 percent per year during the Bush administration, faster than the spending increase. As a result all of the incremental outlays and some of the outlays for continuing programs were financed by borrowing. The 10.7 percent annual growth in the debt during the Bush administration was virtually unchanged from the growth in the Reagan period after accounting for differences in inflation (see Table 7-1).

Signs were increasing that the debt was choking economic growth and retarding any improvement in American living standards. GDP grew at an average nominal dollar rate of 4.7 percent per year under Bush, which was a rate of only 0.6 percent after netting out the 4.1 percent inflation rate. The inflation-adjusted growth rate averaged a minus 1.6 percent during the Carter presidency and a plus 2.3 percent during the Reagan presidency. Living standards were in essence stagnant under Bush and spending proposals were confronted with the response that the government was without the resources to finance certain programs, even those that involved national security. For example, at the outset of the Gulf War with Iraq, the United States sought and received contributions from major allies to pay their share of the war's costs.

The recession in the early 1990s during which the GDP growth was negative and the long good-bye that followed reflected the inadequacy of productive investments and capital formation for more than a decade. This forcefully emphasized that the income tax system was not suitable. When Bush failed to obtain the capital gains tax reduction he presented to Congress early in his term the signal was clear. But he seemed unable to interpret the message and did not come forward with measures to stimulate capital formation and deal with the debt, nor did he propose other measures to stimulate the economy, which slowly came to a standstill.

Had the capital markets been free from the Carter-era inflationary spiral and a distortionary tax system, economic output would have been higher and likewise tax revenues. Instead, the federal government in the 1990s became the not-so-proud owner of thousands of empty office buildings, residences and hotels to say nothing about the deficit-financed spending to pay for depositor losses in failed thrifts.

The Bush Response to the Debt Crisis

By the end of 1990 GRH was no longer taken seriously by Congress or the Bush administration. Congress could not pass a federal budget for fiscal year 1991 that was acceptable to the Bush White House. The process had completely deadlocked. In desperation, President Bush and Congressional leaders turned in December of 1990, to "budget summitry". Perhaps the most memorable outcome of this budget summit was that President Bush broke his pledge on taxes, which was the key theme of his 1988 campaign. In addition, the budget accord placed spending ceilings on major budget categories (defense, domestic discretionary spending, and so forth). No funds could be reallocated between budget categories which meant that any increase in spending within a category had to be made by eliminating another program in that category. The thinking at the time was apparently to protect the defense budget from being cut in order to fund expansion of nondefense activities. If defense spending were cut, the savings would then go towards deficit reduction.

The 1990 budget accord lasted just over a year but could not withstand a combination of three forces: the collapse of the Soviet Union as a military threat, the severe economic recession that began in the spring of 1991, and the 1992 presidential elections. But the administration's problems were far broader than simply a breakdown of this budget agreement: an ill-advised president declared the recession was over. The economic downturn was treated as a normal fluctuation in the business cycle that would work its way to adjustment. With the presidential election approaching Bush adopted an ambivalent posture. Even his State of the Union message in January 1992 offered no bold programs. It was late in his term. Perhaps an attack on the fundamental problem was considered untimely, or perhaps he viewed the current economic dislocations concerning such things as unemployment and stagnant growth as temporary. Bush, like Carter and Reagan before him, gave little recognition of the need for structural change. With Bush it also appeared to be a case of disinclination to rock the boat. Such wishful thinking has rarely been kindly rewarded.

The recession was persistent. It had been long in the making, and its roots were structural. For these reasons, which were not well identified by the authorities both political and economic, it was deeper and longer than most had either recognized or predicted.

At the close of the Bush administration the national debt had climbed to $3.4 trillion, a 43 percent increase since it came into office in 1989.

COMMENTARY

Several lessons from the Carter-to-Reagan-to-Bush transition should be clear. During the tenure of these three administrations that embraced fiscally conservative views, including the need for a balanced budget and an aversion to federal borrowing, America experienced the largest increase in national debt in its peacetime history. And unlike the wartime episodes in America's past where a large debt was incurred, the debt incurred during these administrations showed no indication of going down, rather it showed a great certainty of going up. The force of the debt as if governed by the physical laws of mass defied ideological promises and prescriptions to eliminate it.

Using the income tax system as a tool for controlling spending has had the disastrous effect of distorting the flow of Americans' savings away from productive investments. Markets for financial capital require years of fiscal stability to function properly. Cavalier changes in the income tax code to appease pressure groups may be smart politics but they do not provide the means for an efficient channeling of funds for investments that create future jobs and lift the standard of living. A stubborn fact is that efficient capital markets operate with a long time frame, exceeding the length of terms for political offices. What better illustration than the boom in the real estate market, enticed by Carter and Reagan policies, that created a crisis more than a decade later.

Attempts to solve the fiscal crises during the three administrations did not hold enduring solutions. In each instance there was a failure to recognize the fundamental nature of the problem, and the intended solutions faltered. As with the GRH legislation in the Reagan years, short-term political forces inevitably overpowered agreements that lacked an inescapable enforcement mechanism. As agreement after agreement to balance the budget has been broken, it should now be evident that fiscal order cannot presently be attained without a significant structural change in fiscal institutions.

A specific plan to create a new institutional structure within which the national debt can be retired is proposed in Chapter 10. The measures that are proposed were influenced in fundamental respects by the Carter-to-Reagan-to-Bush period in American politics. Their responses to the debt crisis were plainly inadequate. And because these three administrations failed to bring forth measures for structural changes to resolve the fundamental problems of the debt and capital formation, the country has not been on a sufficiently productive course. Drastic remedial measures must now be pursued.

The national necessity for a system requiring structural changes to promote incentives to save and to encourage capital formation and debt reduction, was accorded all too little action during these administrations. Carter wanted to make some changes but his efforts were inconsequential. During the Reagan administration there were two stabs at revising the income tax system, and they missed the mark. Bush's efforts to revise the capital gains tax were knocked down by Congress and his administration should have learned from the growing inability of the government to finance the federal budget that revolutionary changes were paramount.

NOTES

[1]Fortunately Operation Desert Storm was neither extensive nor costly for the U.S. during the Bush administration. Financial commitments to the United States from foreign governments paid for most of that war's costs.

[2]Michael Evans, *The Truth about Supply-Side Economics* (New York: Basic Books), 1983.

[3]Glenn Pascall, *The Trillion Dollar Budget* (Seattle: University of Washington Press), 1985, p. 23. and Michael Evans, *op. cit.*, p. 11.

[4] *National Journal*, February 22, 1992, p. 439.

[5]Calculations made from data in Council of Economic Advisors, *Economic Report of the President, 1987*, p. 251.

[6]Bureau of Labor Statistics, cited in the "Harper's Index", *Harper's* (September 1986), p. 11.

[7]See discussion on behavior of real wages in Chapter 4.

8

Past Experience
in Debt Repayment:
Ethical Commitment
of the Founders

> The payment of the debt is the great dogma of the
> democratic principle. The discharge of the debt is
> vital to the destiny of our government, ... [1]

In contrast to some of the later presidents, the first five
presidents who played such an important role in the colonial
era and in the founding of the United States, clearly understood the consequences of governmental debt and made
courageous and successful efforts to repay it. In surveying
the early financial history of the United States, two very
important points stand out: (1) the American people had ex-
pended a large sum of money, in addition to lives, in order
to establish their nation, much of which was financed by
borrowing; and (2) the national debt that was incurred in financing the war for independence was paid. It is significant,
therefore, to observe that the initial American experience
with its national debt was long-sighted, prudent, and most
successful.

THE REVOLUTIONARY WAR'S COST

The pursuit of the Revolutionary War cost the colonies an estimated $535 million. This included $5 million of the expenditures spent abroad, $21 million expended by the states, $17 million for supplies, and $492 million for wages and supplies paid for in cash. Not included in this cost was an estimated $50 million spent by France during the course of the 5 year war.[2] When George Washington was inaugurated as the first president of the United States, he presided over a national debt of over $75 million. The population, capital stock, and land area of the nation were small, and one may refer to this period as a time of debt without credit. On the basis of the first census that was taken in the United States in 1790, the population was four million, and thus the debt amounted to about $20 per man, woman, and child.[3] That was a staggering sum for the people of the young republic.

Under the Articles of Confederation, Congress had no taxing power; war financing was based on printing the Continental and State paper currencies and on borrowing. In 1783 Alexander Hamilton realized the problem of war financing, and pointed out many defects of the Articles of Confederation. One of which, as Hamilton wrote, was:

> Indeed, in authorizing Congress at all to emit an *unfunded* paper as the sign of value, a resource which though useful in the infancy of this country, and indispensable in the commencement of the revolution, ought not to continue a formal part of the Constitution, nor ever, hereafter, to be employed, being, in its nature, pregnant with abuses, and liable to be made the engine of imposition and fraud, holding out temptations equally pernicious to the integrity of government and to the morals of the people.

Hamilton then proceeded to persuade Congress to enact legislation whereby the United States would accept responsibility for the debt incurred during the Revolutionary War. This debt, of course, could have been repudiated because the United States as an entity did not exist when the war debt was incurred. However, assumption of the war debt by the new nation signaled an ethic of responsibility that established its financial honor and created the expectation of future reliability.

The financial ethic of the Founders symbolized by their actions to repay the war debt was vital to the future growth and economic success of the nation. The transformation of America from a poor agrarian economy into a diversified industrial nation was dependent on its ability to attract considerable amounts of capital. This capital was forthcoming, which was the key ingredient in the development of a dynamic manufacturing sector and industrial capacity. The Founders of the newly created government established the nation's reputation for financial responsibility and integrity, and this was the foundation for progress.

THE DEBT AND ITS REPAYMENT

The Constitution, which replaced the Articles of Confederation, gave Congress the specific power "to lay and collect taxes, duties, imports, and excises to pay the debts and provide for the common defense and general welfare of the United States". In September 1789, the Treasury Department was established, and Alexander Hamilton, still in his early thirties, became the first Treasury Secretary. The new Congress turned its attention to the problem of repaying the debt. Of the total debt, $10 million was foreign debt with accrued interest of $1.6 million. About two-thirds of this was owed to France, one-third to Holland, and a negligible $174,000 to Spain.[4] In 1793, with some controversy, the federal government also assumed the states' war debts of $18.2 million.[5]

Repayment of the Revolutionary War debt began with Secretary Hamilton's obtaining authorization from Congress for the refunding and repayment of the debt. Hamilton followed a British model and established a "sinking fund" (the so-called Pitt Plan) that was based on the principle that compound interest would make a relatively small endowment grow rapidly into a much larger one in order to pay the debt. Hamilton's sinking fund was to receive surplus revenue from the federal government's budget. The sinking fund was established by a Congressional act on August 12, 1790 and was extended by a second act on May 8, 1792. The money that was appropriated to set this fund in operation was obtained from borrowings of less than $2 million, which the president was authorized to make. Some of this debt was sold in Holland. Finally, an act on March 3, 1795, gave formal existence to a sinking fund that was financed by:

1. The revenue of imports and tonnage as, together with moneys already at the disposal of the Fund commissioners, was necessary to make an annual two percent payment upon the principal of the six percent stock for which the government was, in 1796, liable.

2. Dividends on bank stock subscribed by the United States.

3. Sums from current revenue equal to the accruing interest on public stock previously purchased or redeemed.

4. New proceeds from the sale of public lands.

5. All moneys received by the United States on account of debts.

6. All surplus moneys remaining in the Treasury at the close of any calendar year.[6]

In a January 21, 1795 report, Hamilton criticized the "progressive accumulation of debt which must ultimately endanger all governments". He advocated "a fundamental maxim . . . that the creation of debt should always be accompanied with the means of extinguishment; this is the true secret for rendering public credit immortal". As such, Hamilton's rule would be that whenever the government issues a debt obligation, it must impose a tax to cover the repayment of this debt.[7]

Hamilton's sinking fund soon became a controversial issue as its administrative machinery became complicated: the fund had gradually become involved in paying debts and borrowing at the same time. Generally speaking, though devoted to paying the debt, Hamilton had succeeded mainly in refunding part of the debt but not in its actual reduction. The small Spanish debt was completely liquidated within a few years. The French debt matured in 1791 and was converted into a dollar debt with a 9 year maturity and a higher rate of interest. It was not possible to convert the Dutch debt due in 1795 from florins to dollars.[8] By the end of President Washington's term in 1795, the total debt had risen to nearly $81 million, as compared to $75 million in 1791.

The terms of Washington's immediate successors were eventful years. The federal budgets during the presidency of John Adams ran surpluses during 3 years of his administration. Nevertheless by 1800, with the end of the Federalist administrations under President Adams, public debt had risen to nearly $83 million (see Table 8-1). It was under Adams' successor, President Thomas Jefferson, and his able Treasury Secretary, Albert Gallatin, that substantial progress was made in extinguishing the debt. Gallatin insisted that the debt be repaid as rapidly as possible by cutting expenses, especially those of the Army and the Navy. He estimated that the debt in 1801 was $83 million and could be reduced by 46 percent in 8 years. It would be almost completely paid off by 1870 if annual appropriations of $7.2 million were provided for the repayment of principal and interest.[9] Gallatin did not abolish Hamilton's sinking fund because he did not want to upset "the plan already adopted for the payment of debts" but he undertook to simplify its mechanism. The fund was to be financed by a permanent appropriation of $7.3 million (which was increased to $8 million because of the loan for the Louisiana Purchase). The appropriated fund was devoted *only* to the paying of the public debt.

Thus, under Mr. Gallatin, an effective policy of debt repayment was established. It consisted of the establishment of a permanent appropriation for the service of the debt that was to pay both interest and principal. Such a fund need not be "inviolable" as called for in Hamilton's sinking fund. On the other hand, Gallatin built into it a certain degree of flexibility: the government should have the liberty in times of an emergency to divert money held in the fund for the payment of debt in order to support new loans. In the Gallatin

TABLE 8-1

NATIONAL DEBT AND DEBT REPAYMENT AFTER THE REVOLUTIONARY WAR

(In millions of dollars)

President	Year	National Debt	Increase or Decrease(-)[1]
Washington		n.a.	n.a.
Washington	1790	n.a	n.a.
Washington	1791	75.463	n.a.
Washington	1792	77.228	1.765
Washington	1793	80.359	3.131
Washington	1794	78.427	-1.932
Washington	1795	80.748	2.321
Washington	1796	83.762	3.014
John Adams	1797	82.064	-1.698
John Adams	1798	79.229	-2.835
John Adams	1799	78.409	-0.820
John Adams	1800	82.976	4.567
Jefferson	1801	83.038	0.062
Jefferson	1802	80.713	-2.325
Jefferson	1803	77.055	-3.658
Jefferson	1804	86.427	9.372
Jefferson	1805	82.312	-4.115
Jefferson	1806	75.723	-6.489
Jefferson	1807	69.218	-6.505
Jefferson	1808	65.196	-4.022
Madison	1809	57.023	-8.173
Madison	1810	53.173	-3.850
Madison	1811	48.006	-5.167
Madison	1812	45.210	-2.796
Madison	1813	55.963	10.753
Madison	1814	81.488	25.525
Madison	1815	99.834	18.346
Madison	1816	127.335	27.501
Madison	1816	127.335	27.501
Monroe	1817	123.492	-3.843
Monroe	1818	103.467	-20.025
Monroe	1819	95.530	-7.937
Monroe	1820	91.016	-4.514
Monroe	1821	89.987	-1.029
Monroe	1822	93.547	3.560
Monroe	1823	90.876	-2.671
Monroe	1824	90.270	-0.606
John Quincy Adams	1825	83.788	-6.482
John Quincy Adams	1826	81.054	-2.734
John Quincy Adams	1827	73.987	-7.067
John Quincy Adams	1828	67.475	-6.512
Jackson	1829	58.421	-9.054
Jackson	1830	48.565	-9.856
Jackson	1831	39.123	-9.442
Jackson	1832	24.322	-14.801
Jackson	1833	7.012	-17.310
Jackson	1834	4.760	-2.252
Jackson	1835	0.038	-4.722
Jackson	1836	0.038	0.000

Source: *Bureau of the Census, Historical Statistics of the U.S.; Colonial Times to 1970* (Washington, D.C.: U.S. Government Printing Office, 1970).

[1]In official statistics this column is presented as "Deficit."

formula, the U.S. sinking fund departed substantially from the English model in the sense that the mechanism for debt repayment became clearer and simpler.[10] With strong support from Jefferson, Gallatin was able to repay a substantial part of the national debt by the end of Jefferson's second administration. As Table 8-1 shows, the debt had diminished by $22 million, from $83 million in 1801 to $57 million in 1809, or by 31 percent. That was in spite of the purchase of the Louisiana Territory in 1804 under Jefferson.

Mr. Jefferson's successor, President Madison, was faced with the War of 1812 and presided over 4 years of continued deficits, reversing the surplus trend of his first 3 years. By 1818 Madison was successful in reducing the debt from $57 million to $45 million, which was about 5 percent of national income. As the war escalated, so did the national debt. By 1816, President Madison's final year of office, the debt had reached $124 million or about 13 percent of national income.

Madison's successors, Presidents James Monroe, John Quincy Adams, and Andrew Jackson, ran substantial and continuous budgetary surpluses (with the exception of 1822, when a deficit of $3.6 million was recorded). With these surpluses, the national debt was steadily diminished. From 1823 to 1835, the national debt repayment effort was uninterrupted. To a large extent, the debt was paid with surplus revenues coming from customs receipts and the sale of public lands (see Table 8-1).

COMMENTARY

The fiscal prudence and the firm resolve of the Founding Fathers had helped to pay off the debts of the Revolutionary War within a relatively short time period. In addition, the prosperity following the war brought in relatively high government revenues that could be applied to paying off the debt. An astounding four-fifths of all federal revenue was devoted to the service of the debt in the decade 1790-1800.[11] By 1835, under President Jackson, all the debts of the Revolutionary War and the War of 1812, totaling $127 million had been completely retired.

It was indeed an historical event of major proportion to record that during the 2 years, 1835 and 1836, the national debt of the United States was practically zero. There was even some surplus to distribute among the states.[12] Much credit for prudent fiscal management must be given to Albert Gallatin. For his wisdom in public finance, especially his advocacy of a permanent appropriation for debt service and reduction of the outstanding principle, made this objective attainable. Gallatin's formula to pay the Revolutionary War debt could have been more successful and the debt paid faster had it not been for the War of 1812 and the following years, which created a substantial increase in the amount of government debt outstanding.

A simple sinking fund as conceived by Gallatin constituted a firm and permanent appropriation by the Congress for the specific purpose of debt repayment. This idea deserves close attention as a mechanism applicable in solving the gargantuan problem presented by the national debt.

NOTES

[1]These were Thomas Jefferson's words to his Treasury Secretary, Albert Gallatin, in October 1809, when Gallatin was experiencing great difficulty confronting the debt problem cited in Henry C. Adams, *Public Debts* (New York: Arno Press, 1975), p. 266.

[2]Margaret G. Myers, *A Financial History of the United States* (New York: Columbia University Press, 1970), 50–51.

[3]*Ibid.*, p. 62.

[4]*Ibid.*, p. 60.

[5]*Ibid.*, p. 62.

[6]Henry C. Adams, *op. cit.*, p. 264.

[7]*Ibid.*, pp. 264–265.

[8]Myers, *op. cit.*, p. 63.

[9]*Ibid.*, p. 64.

[10]See Adams, *op. cit.*, pp. 268–269.

[11]Myers, *op. cit.*, p. 62.

[12]Committee on Public Debt Policy, *op. cit.*, p. 12.

9

Debt Repayment after the Civil War, World War I, and World War II

NATIONAL DEBT REPAYMENT EXPERIENCE AFTER THE CIVIL WAR

The determination of national leaders and the successful payment of the national debt after the Civil War was another shining experience in the financial history of the United States; an experience that sheds some light on our current debt problems and offers guidance for resolution.

The Cost of the Civil War

As in many wartime periods, a combination of factors resulted in an explosion of the national debt. The Civil War lasted longer and the conflict was more intense than had been expected, which resulted in a tremendous drain on the Treasury. Poor financial management by the Treasury as well as the inability of Congress to provide adequate taxation resulted in revenue shortfalls. The federal government relied heavily on borrowing, and the national debt, which was $65 million in 1860, soared to $2.8 billion in 1866, 1 year after the war ended. Of this, some $600 million was in the form of paper money called greenbacks. The contributing

factors to the staggering national debt were summarized by
a noted economist, Barton Hepburn, as follows:

> Utter failure to foresee the probable length and
> magnitude of the war, hence failure to provide
> largely increased taxation, always unpalatable to
> short-sighted legislators; first resort to note-issues
> rendered necessary by the absence of a reputable
> currency system and of credit abroad through
> which specie could be drawn; the vain desire not to
> see bonds at a discount, and consequent inability to
> sell them as rapidly as needs arose; wretched mili-
> tary administration and waste in innumerable
> ways; suspension of coin payments precipitated by
> unwise management and foreign complications;
> forced legal tender currency loans and expansion
> of prices, checking commodity exports and increa-
> sing expenses; heavy exports of specie naturally
> following; more legal tender currency, with further
> rise in prices and increases in expenses; repudi-
> ation of right to fund legal tender notes into bonds;
> while speculation in specie, which extended into all
> lines of business, enriching the shrewd few at the
> expense of the many. Net result — ultimate cost to
> the people very much more than it would have
> been had they been taxed more heavily at the out-
> set.[1]

Consequently, the $2.8 billion debt, or 50.2 percent of the
national income, was borne by a country that was still small
in population and land. On a per capita basis, the debt rose
from $15 after the War of 1812 to nearly $78 after the Civil
War.

To Pay or Not to Pay

At the end of the Civil War there were three competing
lines of thought regarding the problem of the national debt:
(1) to convert the debt into fiat paper money; (2) to make the
debt a permanent feature and reduce it gradually; or (3) to
pay it quickly. Fortunately enough, the American people,
who had been accustomed to high government borrowing

during the Civil War, turned around completely to demand a quick payment of the debt. Commenting on the episode, the secretary of the British Legation had this to say:

> The majority of Americans would appear disposed to endure any amount of sacrifice rather than leave any portion of their debt to future generations.[2]

Another observer, historian Albert Bolles, said:

> From the first, the policy of national debt paying has been widely favored. Some interests which would be better served by continuing the debt has sought to reverse this policy, but the voice of the people has been quite unanimous.[3]

Professor Robert T. Patterson, a noted author on the history of debt management, wrote of this period:

> In some areas of public opinion the American debt situation was compared with that of the British, by which, it was supposed, the British people had long been oppressed. ... Direct robbery by force could not have obtained this (oppression) so effectually as has been done through the creation of a permanent national debt.[4]

Because of the attitude of the American people, which favored a quick elimination of the debts, the administrations during the postwar years were able to reduce the debt. The experience in this period deserves to be examined carefully.

Level and Structure of the Debts

The national debt increased dramatically from 1861 to 1865 as shown in Table 9-1. It was reported that about $600 million of this debt was held by Europeans. By the middle of 1866, the debt reached its peak of $2.8 billion, which consisted of various types of debt (see Table 9-1). Of the total,

TABLE 9-1
NATIONAL DEBT, 1861-1865

Year	1861	1862	1863	1864	1865
Issued	489.3	776.5	1,128.9	1,475.0	3.869.7
Redeemed	51.7	181.0	432.9	603.4	1,269.0
Net Increase	437.6	595.5	696.0	871.6	2,600.7

Source: Patterson, p. 45; Appendix 1.

$684 million were legal tender: U.S. notes, 5 percent notes, and compound interest notes. Interest to service the $2.8 billion debt reached 2.6 percent of national income at war's end.

Debt Payment

It was estimated at the time that between 27 to 32 years were needed to pay this debt.[5] As it turned out, in 28 years a substantial portion of the debt (65 percent) had been liquidated.

From the outset, President Andrew Johnson had opposed a permanent debt so vehemently that he advocated its repudiation. He proposed that interest payments be counted as payments of principal.[6] Fortunately, he left the matter to his able Treasury Secretary, Mr. Hugh McCulloch, who resolved that the debt must be paid:

> There can be no reasonable doubt that a national debt is a national burden, for which there can be no substantial counterbalancing compensations.[7]

That the debt was a national burden that must be discharged was a policy which McCulloch faithfully pursued during his entire tenure from 1866 to 1869. First, committing himself to a policy of debt conversion, then to its contraction. As shown in Table 9-2, less than half of the $2.8 billion national debt in 1866 was funded debt; about $1.7 billion had been issued using a grab-bag of other debt instruments. In April 1866, McCulloch requested and received authority from Congress to convert much of the unfunded debt into more manageable funded debt. By the middle of 1868, he reported that $1 billion of the temporary obligations had been converted into funded debt. The success of conversion and the elimination of greenbacks had prepared the foundation for McCulloch and his successors to move rapidly to reduce the debt.[8]

Consequently, within 7 years the debt that had swollen during the Civil War years was reduced by $600 million, or 22 percent, from $2.8 billion in 1866 to $2.2 billion in 1873 (Table 9-2). By 1873, however, the nation went through a

TABLE 9-2
PEAK CIVIL WAR DEBT, 1866

Funded debt	$1,109,568,191.80
Matured debt	1,503,020.09
Temporary loans	107,148,713.16
Certificates of indebtedness	85,093,000.00
Five percent legal tender notes	33,954,230.00
Compound interest legal tender notes	217,024,160.00
Seven-thirty notes	830,000,000.00
United States notes (legal tenders)	433,160,569.00
Fractional currency	26,344,742.51
Suspended requisitions uncalled for	2,111,000.00
Total	$2,845,907,626.56
Deduct cash in Treasury	88,218,055.13
Balance	$2,757,689,571.43

Source: *Treasury Report*, 1867.

crisis called "the panic of 1873", and a depression in the following 5 years complicated the debt payment effort. If it had not been for this depression during which economic output declined and tax revenues fell, payment of the debt would have been faster. It should be noted that during these years, there was the relatively large federal expenditure for the purchase of Alaska in 1867. In spite of all this, by 1893 the debt had been reduced to $961 million. Sixty-five percent of the debt had been fully paid, and nearly all the callable part of the debt had been called and paid.

In the following year, 1894, there was another depression, deeper than that of 1873-1878, which lasted until 1899, and the debt was increased to $1.4 billion. Some payments were made in the following years, and the debt was stabilized at approximately $1 billion until World War I. The national debt, which was 50.2 percent of income in 1865, was only 7 percent in 1893. As a result, per capita debt, which stood at $78 in 1865, was reduced to a mere $7 in 1893.

How Was It Possible?

The success of debt payment after the Civil War was achieved not only by prudent fiscal policy and economic prosperity, but by the determination of the American people and their leaders to eliminate the debt. The American people, accustomed to higher than normal taxes during the Civil War years, continued to tolerate a high tax burden to extinguish the national debt in the war's aftermath. The *London Economist* commented:

> In any other country the mere attempt [to continue such a heavy tax] would have caused a revolution, but in America these taxes are borne as patiently as taxes are ever borne in any country. . . . Congress simply laid a tax on everything it could think of and let it hit whom it could. Yet this financial decimation of the people excites little murmuring.[9]

Because of the general public's readiness to bear high taxes in order to pay the debt, Congress reduced taxes only gradually over the years. Immediately after the Civil War, Treasury Secretary McCulloch in 1866 advocated that government revenues should be maintained at a level high enough to generate adequate funds in order to reduce the principal of the debt by $4 million to $5 million per month.[10] He estimated that the debt would reach $3 billion at its peak, which would require about $150 million per year to pay interest.[11] Consequently, McCulloch proposed that Congress appropriate $200 million per year to service the debt. If

Congress had followed this recommendation the total debt would have been paid off in about 28 years. Nevertheless, Congress did not adopt the McCulloch proposal.[12]

How, then, was the Civil War debt retired? Simply out of the budget surpluses which the federal government had experienced annually from 1866 to 1879. A substantial part of these surpluses were derived from the high tariff that was imposed during the Civil War that had continued into the postwar years. The average rate of tariff was 47 percent on all dutiable commodities. McCulloch later commented in his memoirs:

> This much must be said in praise of the United States Tariff Act of 1862, that by the high duties which it imposed and the taxes on whiskey and tobacco, etc., more than one-half of the United States' debt had been paid. ... The country is indebted to protective tariff for the rapid reduction of the public debt.[13]

The Sinking Fund

The original sinking fund was established during and after the Revolutionary War as discussed in Chapter 8. During the Civil War, another sinking fund was established by the Capital Loan Act of February 25, 1862, under which import duties were to be dedicated to pay interest on the debt and then to purchase or make payment of "1 percent of the entire debt of the United States, to be made within each fiscal year. ... which is to be set apart as a sinking fund, and the interest of which shall in like manner be applied".[14] Nevertheless, after the war, Treasury Secretary McCulloch ignored the fund and argued that "the safe and simple way of sinking the national debt is to apply directly to its payment the excess of receipts over expenditures".[15]

In 1869, President Grant's Treasury Secretary, Mr. George S. Boutwell, revived the sinking fund, and on July 14, 1870, Congress enacted the Refunding Act, reestablishing the fund.[16] Nevertheless, the fund was oversimplified, and it was a very controversial issue. As Professor Patterson put it, the sinking fund had become "a false aid to those financiers who would rely upon it".[17] Or as Professor Ross stated: "No financial task has so befooled statesmen and led to costly mistakes as the 'sinking' of public debt."[18] The weaknesses of a sinking fund appear when it is operated to assume functions separate from the debt it was created to service. As Charles Bastable, one of the first and foremost writers on public finance, commented:

> The whole history of the "sinking-fund" doctrine is an illustration of this tendency. In its earlier form the sinking fund was simply the surplus of certain parts of the public revenue set apart for the discharge of debt, and derived all its efficacy from the excess of revenue expenditure. But very soon, the fund was transformed from being a part of the financial mechanism, to a positive entity, and treated as if it had an independent existence. On its security, fresh loans were contracted and the absurdity of borrowing with one hand while repaying with the other was frequently perpetrated.[19]

In addition to these weaknesses, the sinking fund also encountered the problem of inflexibility; it required the same amount of inflow of funds (e.g., the same appropriation) in each and every year, even in times of recession. When government revenues were very low, they were not adequate to meet the requirements of the fund. Generally speaking, it was not the sinking fund that made the Civil War debt payment successful; rather, it was exactly excellence in budgetary management by which surpluses were produced.

Finally, 65 percent of that part of the national public debt incurred for the Civil War was repaid by 1893. If it had not been for the depression years of 1873 to 1878, the debt would probably have been paid in 28 years as predicted by Mr. McCulloch. The large reduction of the debt was mainly attributable to the determination of the American people and their leaders to devote budget surpluses to debt repayment, as opposed to new federal programs. Such determination was surely driven by an ethic that regarded debt as a burden that ought not be transferred to future generations. The champion of that effort, Secretary McCulloch, commented in his memoirs: "That the reduction should have been commenced within seven months from the close of a war of unequaled cost, and continued through years of great financial depression, is about the last thing that the advocates or supporters of monarchy expected from a republican government".[20] Civil War debt repayment yields a lesson we could learn on the method of debt repayment. Debt repayment is best achieved by establishing an adequate revenue source and dedicating that revenue and any annual surpluses solely to debt retirement.

DEBT PAYMENT EXPERIENCE OF WORLD WAR I AND WORLD WAR II

As pointed out earlier, a substantial part of the cost of the Civil War, about two-thirds, was paid by 1893. By that time, however, depression had set in, and again the country went through years of budget deficits. As a consequence, the national debt rose dramatically between 1894 and 1899. In 1899 under President McKinley, the debt was $1.4 billion. Both Presidents McKinley and Theodore Roosevelt made commendable, though modest, efforts to reduce the debts without interruption from 1900 to 1905. From 1906 until the outbreak of World War I in 1914, the national debt remained fairly stable at about $1.2 billion.

The Turning Point

The turning point in the history of the national debt took place at the outbreak of World War I. The total cost of the war from 1914 to 1920 was estimated at $82 billion for all parties, of which the United States alone incurred a net cost estimated at $23 billion, excluding about $10 billion in loans to allies.[21] As shown in Table 9-3, between 1916 and 1919 wartime financing increased the debt twentyfold to $25.5 billion.

TABLE 9-3
NATIONAL DEBT AND DEBT REPAYMENT AFTER
  WORLD WAR I
(in millions of dollars)

President	Year	National Debt	Increase or Decrease(-)
Wilson	1913	1,193.048	-0.791
Wilson	1914	1,188.235	-4.813
Wilson	1915	1,191.264	3.029
Wilson	1916	1,225.146	33.882
Wilson	1917	2,975.619	1,750.473
Wilson	1918	12,455.225	9,479.606
Wilson	1919	25,484.506	13,029.281
Wilson	1920	24,299.321	-1,185.185
Harding	1921	23,977.451	-321.870
Harding	1922	22,963.382	-1,014.069
Coolidge	1923	22,349.707	-613.675
Coolidge	1924	21,250.813	-1,098.894
Coolidge	1925	20,516.194	-734.619
Coolidge	1926	19,643.216	-872.978
Coolidge	1927	18,511,907	-1,131.309
Coolidge	1928	17,604.293	-907.614
Hoover	1929	16,931.088	-673.205
Hoover	1930	16,185.310	-745.778

Source: Bureau of the Census, *Historical Statistics of the U.S.: Colonial Times to 1970* (Washington, D.C.: U.S. Government Printing Office, 1975).

As soon as the war was over, President Wilson immediately began the urgent task of paying the national debt. In 1919, another sinking fund was established under which World War I debt (excluding foreign loans) was to be retired within 25 years.[22] In 1920 alone, the first year after the war, nearly $1.2 billion of Treasury revenues were used to pay off the debt. President Wilson's efforts opened the way for his successors, Presidents Harding and Coolidge, to continue to retire the debt. As a result, by 1930 nearly $10 billion of the debt, or 36 percent of the 1919 level, had been paid (see Table 9-3). Details of the way the debt was paid are shown in Table 9-4. Most of the funds to retire the debt came from the excess of government receipts over expenditures reflected in Treasury surpluses and the sinking fund, and from revenue obtained from the sale of government assets acquired by the government during the war (not shown in Table 9-4 but estimated to be about $800 million).[23]

TABLE 9-4
WORLD WAR I PUBLIC DEBT RETIREMENT (1919-1930)

	Amount	Percent
Gross debt outstanding, June 30, 1919	25,482,034,418.49	-
Debt reduction From Treasury surpluses	3,476,729,404.93	37.40
Sinking fund	3,187,468,300.00	34.29
Debt payments by foreign governments	1,488,720,450.00	16.01
Reduction in balance of general fund	913,382,020.23	9.82
Miscellaneous	230,425,944.15	2.48
	9,296,726,119.31	100.00
Gross debt outstanding, June 30, 1930	16,185,308,299.18	

After the tremendous success with the debt retirement, the country entered the "Great Depression" years starting in 1929. From 1930 until the outbreak of World War II, the national debt rose dramatically once again. By 1940 the debt rose to nearly $43 billion, and in 1944 the sinking fund purchase was discontinued.[24]

WORLD WAR II

The outlay of expenditures for World War II was ten times higher than World War I. Of this expenditure, 58 percent was financed by borrowing.[25] The national debt reached a peak of nearly $270 billion in the middle of 1946 (see Table 9-5).

TABLE 9-5
NATIONAL DEBT AND DEBT REPAYMENT
AFTER WORLD WAR II
(in millions of dollars)

President	Year	National Debt	Increase or Decrease(-)
Roosevelt	1940	42,967.531	2,427.999
Roosevelt	1941	48,961.444	5,993.913
Roosevelt	1942	72,422.445	23,461.001
Roosevelt	1943	136,696.090	64,273.645
Roosevelt	1944	201,003.387	64,307.297
Roosevelt	1945	258,682.187	57,678.180
Truman	1946	269,422.009	10,739.912
Truman	1947	258,286.383	-11,135.716
Truman	1948	252,292.247	-5,994.136
Truman	1949	252,770.360	478.113
Truman	1950	257,357.352	4,586.992
Truman	1951	255,221.977	-2,135.375
Truman	1952	259,105.179	3,883.202
Eisenhower	1954	271,259.599	5,188.537
Eisenhower	1955	274,374.223	3,114.624
Eisenhower	1956	272,750.814	-1,623.409
Eisenhower	1957	270,527.172	-2,223.642

Source: Bureau of the Census, *Historical Statistics of the U.S.: Colonial Times to 1970* (Washington, D.C.: U.S. Government Printing Office, 1975).

During World War II it was the Treasury's policy to borrow on short maturity where interest rates were lower and thus maintain a low cost for debt service. One result of this policy was an increase in the proportion of the debt that was of short maturity. At the end of 1945, debt of short-term maturity (bills, certificates, and notes) accounted for 41 percent of marketable issues (see Table 9-6) as compared to only 23 percent in 1940.[26]

With increasingly greater debt of short-term duration, the Treasury was required to refund continuously, a costly operation that also added uncertainty to financial markets. This development is significant because it initiated a trend in policy toward relying on debt deferral coupled with refunding, a trend in policy in debt management policy that has persisted.

TABLE 9-6
NATIONAL DEBT AT THE END OF WORLD WAR II: MARKETABLE ISSUES
(in millions of dollars)

	Bills, Certificates and Notes	Bonds	Total
Federal Reserve bank	23.3	1.0	24.3
Commercial bank	36.3	46.5	82.8
Savings banks and insurance companies	1.3	32.4	33.8
Other	17.3	33.6	51.0
TOTAL	78.2	113.5	191.8

Source: *Federal Reserve Bulletin*, March 1946, p. 318. (Reprinted in M. Myers, *op. cit.* p. 351).

Debt Payment

In 1945, Treasury Secretary Henry Morgenthau, Jr. estimated that the cost of World War II to the United States had been $325 billion, or about one-half of the GNP during that period. This can be compared with the cost of World War I, which was one-fourth of the total GNP during the years of that war.[27] When World War II ended, the public sentiment was overwhelmingly in favor of payment of the national debt. Reflecting the mood of the country, the Senate voted 64 to 20 on March 1, 1947 to pay — out of budgetary surpluses — at least $2.6 billion on the national debt in 1948.[28]

During the post-World War II period, President Truman also took immediate steps to reduce the debt. From its peak of $279 billion, which existed in February 1946, the debt decreased by $27 billion to $252 billion in April 1948, a decrease of 10 percent over a period of 26 months. The debt payment was possible because of the excess of Treasury balances built up by the Victory Loan in late 1945. In 1947 and in 1948, a total of $7 billion of the debt was paid, mainly out of budgetary surpluses. Although the Korean conflict halted the progress of the debt payment, President Truman made an effort in 1951 to pay $2.1 billion. Then, under the Eisenhower administration, in spite of all the expenditures to finance the cold war, budget surpluses were recorded in 2 years, 1956 and 1957, and a total of nearly $4 billion of the national debt was paid. After 1957 the national debt fluctuated and gradually receded for two decades to a post-World War II low in 1974 when the debt in relation to GDP bottomed-out at 24.5 percent.

COMMENTARY

Subsequent to 1975 with unbridled growth the debt reached 50 percent of GDP and 121 percent of the domestic savings pool in the 1990s. Serious effort in national debt repayment had become an endeavor of the past. Should this summon to memory Gray's "Elegy Written in a Country Church-Yard"?

> The Curfew tolls the knell of parting day,
> The lowing herd wind slowly o'er the lea,
> The plowman homeward plods his weary way,
> And leaves the world to darkness and to me.[29]

Let us master the lessons of the past and move forward with a plan for national debt retirement.

NOTES

[1]Barton A. Hepburn, *History of Coinage and Currency in the United States and the Perennial Contest for Sound Money* (New York and London: The Macmillan Co., 1903), p. 202.

[2]Francis A. Walker, "The National Debt", *Lippincott's Monthly Magazine*, IV (September 1869), p. 316.

[3]Albert Sydney Bollas, *The Financial History of the U.S. from 1861 to 1885* (New York: D. Appleton and Co., 1886), p. 305.

[4]Robert Patterson, *Federal Debt Management Policies*, 1865-

1879 (Durham: Duke University Press, 1954), p. 57. Patterson's quotation is from "Conversion of the National Debt to Capital." *Lippincott's Monthly Magazine*, I (June 1868), p. 641.

[5]Secretary Hugh McCulloch's "Estimate: 27 to 29 Years" (*Treasury Report, 1865*, pp. 23–25); Freeman Clark, Comptroller of the Currency's estimate: 32 1/2 years (*Report of the Comptroller of the Currency, 1865*, p. 68). See Patterson, *op. cit.*, p. 61.

[6]Robert Patterson, *op. cit.*, p. 61.

[7]Hugh McCulloch, *Men and Measures of Half a Century* (New York: Charles Scribner's Sons, 1888), p. 472.

[8]Margaret G. Myers, *A Financial History of the United States* (New York: Columbia University Press, 1970), pp. 176–179.

[9]*London Economist*, XXIV (December 22, 1866), p. 1481.

[10]*Treasury Report, 1866*, pp. 6–7, 24.

[11]Henry C. Adams, *Public Debts* (New York: Arno Press, 1975), p. 270.

[12]*Ibid*.

[13]Hugh McCulloch, *op. cit.*, p. 473.

[14]Robert Patterson, *op. cit.*, p. 137.

[15]*Ibid.*, p. 138.

[16]Robert Patterson, *op. cit.*, p. 139.

[17]Robert Patterson, *op. cit.*, p. 142.

[18]Edward A. Ross, "Sinking Funds," *Publications of the American Economic Association*, First Series, 1892, Vol. VII, Nos. 4-5, p. 396 (quoted in Patterson, Robert, p. 142).

[19]Charles F. Bastable, *Public Finance* (London and New York: The Macmillan Co. 1892), p. 479.

[20]Hugh McCulloch, *op. cit.*, p. 209.

[21]Margaret G. Myers, *op. cit.*, pp. 291–292.

[22]Committee on Public Debt Policy (New York: Harcourt, Brace and Co., Inc., 1949), p. 34.

[23]*Ibid.*, p. 57.

[24]*Ibid.*, p. 34.

[25]Harold M. Groves, *Financing Government*, 6th ed. (New York: Holt Rinehart and Winston, 1964), p. 352.

[26]Margaret G. Myers, *op. cit.*, p. 350.

[27]*Ibid.*, p. 360.

[28]Committee on Public Debt Policy, *Our National Debt* (New York: Harcourt, Brace and Co., Inc., 1949), p. 31.

[29]Thomas Gray, "Elegy Written in a Country Church-Yard," in *Gray Poetry and Prose* (London: Oxford University Press, 1963), p. 62.

10

The Plan for Debt Retirement

In 1992 the people of America were saddled with a national debt of $4 trillion and with more borrowed money were paying interest annually of $200 billion. But debt principal was not being paid and reduced; it was being continuously refunded. Therein, amounts were borrowed to pay interest and then piled on top of the existing debt, which would become part of principal upon which more interest would be paid. This debt for which neither immediate nor forthright remedial action has been proposed is a formidable barrier to economic improvement for America.

What should be the conclusion of the most serious domestic dilemma this nation has faced since the Civil War?

OVERVIEW OF THE DEBT RETIREMENT PLAN

To be effective and acceptable a program to restore federal fiscal balance must preclude the opportunity for future politicians to violate the plan once initiated. A compact is required to preclude political maneuvering and to endure future attempts to alter its terms. The Plan presented here is one that deprives politicians of discretion to divert into other purposes revenues intended for debt retirement. Congresses and administrations subsequently elected must be bound by the terms of the debt retirement compact. A self-enforcement mechanism to bind future legislators to the

Plan is essential, because, without it, currently enacted legislation will subsequently become disarranged, whatever its merits. This lesson is clearly learned from episodes like the Gramm-Rudman experience of the 1980s.[1]

In contrast to Gramm-Rudman which set *deficit* reduction as its target, this Plan aims directly at retiring the nation's currently outstanding debt. By restructuring the debt and thereby phasing out the interest expense in the budget, the Plan will begin to rectify the deficit problem. For example, the deficit in 1992 would have been reduced to $114 billion from $314 billion without the interest component.

Judging from history, politicians in the United States have consistently honored only one form of fiscal compact, the constitutionally imposed requirement that the government must repay its debts. Interest payments on the national debt are the only constitutionally mandated item in the federal budget. Yet in practice "debt repayment" has not amounted to debt reduction. It has amounted only to a constant refunding of the debt under federal legislation enacted annually to raise the debt limit and provide authority to the Federal Reserve to borrow and refund. Incurring new debt simply to roll over maturing debt will not solve the country's fiscal dilemma. This scheme of continuously deferring and refunding forestalls financial reckoning but at a tremendous and rapidly growing cost. Perpetually rolling over the national debt involves an endless and costly search for participants to furnish resources to perpetuate this game. While the world's supply of financial participants has not run out, the risk of a declining participation increases.

The price of refinancing the national debt is likewise increasing as potential purchasers of U.S. Treasury bonds see a rising risk of repudiation. As previous chapters have documented, the national debt is rising faster than the nation's ability and willingness to pay. Refunding will ultimately become untenable. Before this happens, however, debt restructuring represents the best mechanism to restrain political discretion and preserve fiscal integrity. Even in the worst of times, politicians have not abrogated the constitutional rule that protects lenders to the U.S. Treasury. The explanation for "honoring" this commitment is no mystery, nor is it symbolic of some special political courage: repudiation of debt obligations would be catastrophic. We would like to believe the Treasury pays its debts because of ethical commitment, but a stronger force lies in the fact that the political consequences of repudiation are far worse than the alternative. Each year members of the House and Senate in what has become an automatic charade pass the requisite legislation, and the president signs into law an increase in the federal debt ceiling. The Treasury then borrows to pay off old borrowing.[2]

As the debt burden increases and the risk of some kind of repudiation rises, continued reliance upon fiscal integrity can become foolish. Repudiation can occur in ways other than an outright declaration that federal debt holders will not be paid. The more likely way is to "print money"; that is, the money supply could be inflated by creating dollars with which holders of debt issues would be paid. This maneuver to the extent of the issues involved would monetize the outstanding debt. Quite plainly the Plan proposed for debt retirement requires action before the fiscal credibility of the federal government is too far diminished.

Fundamental Elements of the Plan

The Debt Retirement Plan has four principle elements resting upon a compact of agreement between the federal government and investors. First, outstanding debt securities that are guaranteed by the general funds of the U.S. Treasury would be replaced by newly issued debt retirement bonds through an exchange procedure. Second, an enforcement mechanism becomes operable and binding for both the federal government and holders of the debt retirement bonds upon their issuance and exchange. Such a mechanism furnishes the assurance needed by bond holders to participate in the exchange. Third, the Plan would preclude the possibility that future repayment of the debt retirement bonds would come from yet more borrowing by the federal government. The practice of refunding is eliminated. This is accomplished by explicitly tying the future repayment of the debt retirement bonds to a solely dedicated revenue source to which holders of the bonds shall have sole recourse. Fourth, the plan involves in effect, a one-time exchange that restructures the entire outstanding balance of the national debt. The importance of restructuring all the debt in a single step, as opposed to a gradual restructuring over a series of years, is to establish at once the compact and a correct fiscal policy that eliminates the procedure of perpetual bond re-funding. It would also lower the cost of the Plan. Such a complete exchange would then provide credit markets with a sure signal that the need of the United States to borrow will decline in the long-term and thus improve the terms of exchange for the newly issued bonds.

Restructuring the Debt through an Exchange

The Debt Retirement Plan proposes to issue new federal bonds of sufficient value to replace all outstanding debt obligations. The purpose of relying on a bond exchange, in contrast to implementing a "debt retirement tax" for exam-ple, is to bind future Congresses and administrations to the program. This exchange is the consideration and the mortar of the compact, as it were. Once the terms for repayment of the debt retirement bonds are set, politicians in subsequent periods are obligated by the contractual compact, because breaking the terms would repudiate the commitment made on the new bonds. The federal government might have the power to do this but not the right, to state this proposition in Hofeldian terms. In contrast, a plan that purports to retire the debt with tax revenues alone leaves open a major risk that such revenues would be diverted to other purposes. Under this Plan that cannot happen without creating an actionable breach. Thus issuing debt retirement bonds in exchange for the outstanding debt is a key element of the Plan because it embraces a compelling and durable enforce-ment mechanism.

Single-Purpose, Dedicated Revenue Source

Perhaps the most important element of the Plan would be to create a single-purpose revenue source which could be specifically dedicated to servicing and repaying the debt retirement bonds. Holders of these bonds would not have any recourse to revenues generally available in the U.S. Treasury. This eliminates the power of Congress to repay the debt retirement bonds by more future-period borrowing. The compact erects an explicit arrangement and the newly-issued debt retirement bonds would be repaid solely from the proceeds of the dedicated tax source. Symmetrically, by the explicit terms of the compact with holders of the debt retirement bonds the proceeds from this dedicated tax could not be used for any other purpose.[3]

Provisions to Handle Revenue Surpluses and Shortfalls

No revenues from the dedicated tax would be allowed to accumulate in the form of a temporary surplus. Surplus revenues are to be used to call debt retirement bonds prior to maturity. Surpluses created in the operation of the Social Security Trust Fund function with an adverse effect upon the federal budgetary process. That undesirable condition would not be perpetuated in the Debt Retirement Plan.[4]

If in any fiscal year the revenues from the dedicated tax exceed the amounts needed to pay off bonds maturing during that fiscal year, bonds with future maturities will be called and their payment will be accelerated. Various types of procedures might be devised to implement any call of the bonds. Among these could be an across-the-board method that reduces all outstanding bonds proportionally, or a random selection method that draws "by lot" a sufficient number of outstanding bonds to exhaust any current period surplus.

Further exploration illuminates. Maturities of retirement bonds as scheduled for each fiscal year will have been predicated upon the dedicated tax revenue anticipated for that particular year. The term structure of the bond portfolio would then have been established by the projected flow of annual revenues from the dedicated tax. If the dedicated tax brings in more than was expected and more than enough funds are available to repay bonds at scheduled maturity, the surplus would be used to call and pay off a portion of the remaining outstanding bonds.

A revenue shortfall can be obviated if maturities are suitably structured. But without the cushion of any surplus balances, provision must be made to handle a condition of insufficient revenues. A provision to forestall the problem of a revenue shortfall would be to use two classes of securities: one class issued with fixed maturity dates and another with flexible maturity dates.[5]

Security for the Debt Retirement Bonds

An essential feature of the Plan is to establish an independent collateral resource. The dedicated revenue source that would secure the debt retirement bonds should possess several properties. First, the future flow of revenues generated by the dedicated tax needs to be predictable. The maturity schedule of the special issue bond portfolio must be established when the Plan is initiated and, therefore, accurately anticipates the revenue stream during subsequent fiscal years. Second, taxation of the revenue source should deter economic growth as little as possible. The major purpose of the debt retirement tax is to stimulate the economy, and this purpose could be counterbalanced by taxing corporate and individual initiatives. The broad alternatives are either to tax production or to tax consumption, and both have distortionary effects on the market process. The issue posed is which alternative, a production tax or a consumption tax, would be the least detrimental to economic growth?

Relative to taxes on earnings (e.g., an income tax, a capital gains tax, or a payroll tax), reformation of the tax system by adopting a consumption tax will best promote the productivity and growth objectives of the Debt Retirement Plan. A tax on consumption will encourage more savings, add resources available for investment, and encourage capital formation.[6]

Tax Function in the Debt Retirement Plan

A consumption tax that satisfies these desirable properties is a flat-rate tax on private sector purchases of all goods and services levied at the producer's level. In Table 10-1 gross national sales figures from 1980 to 1990 are used to project the size of this tax base in future years. Gross national sales during the 1980s increased at an average annual rate of 6.25 percent. A simple trend is used to extrapolate values though the year 2003, and to be conservative, it assumes an average annual growth rate of 6 percent. The revenue projections are also shown in Table 10-1. The projected revenue base in the year 1994 is about $5.5 trillion and rises to $9.2 trillion in the year 2003.

TABLE 10-1
PAST AND PROJECTED LEVELS OF U.S. GROSS NATIONAL SALES*

Year	Actual Values in Billions of Current Dollars	Year	Projected Values in Billions of Current Dollars**
1980	$2,210.0	1994	$5,458.7
1981	$2,440.5	1995	$5,786.2
1982	$2,548.8	1996	$6,133.4
1983	$2,737.8	1997	$6,501.4
1984	$2,968.6	1998	$6,891.5
1985	$3,182.8	1999	$7,305.0
1986	$3,352.6	2000	$7,743.3
1987	$3,565.9	2001	$8,207.9
1988	$3,885.0	2002	$8,700.4
1989	$4,146.9	2003	$9,222.4
1990	$4,402.2		

Source: Council of Economic Advisers, Economics Indicators, Washington, D.C. October, 1990.

Notes: *Values are for Total Gross National Sales less Government Purchases of Goods and Services. **Projections assume an average annual growth rate of 6 percent, whereas the actual growth rate for the 1980 to 1990 period was 6.25 percent.

Using the computations in Table 10-1 for the projected size of the tax base, the general parameters are developed for the Debt Retirement Plan. The value of the debt retirement bonds that must be issued and a maturity schedule are estimated, as well as the required tax rate to finance their repayment.

ARCHITECTURE FOR A TEN-YEAR PLAN

Several assumptions make the formulation and analysis of a specific proposal tractable. A variety of adjustments might be suitable in the details that follow and the effects of these are discussed as appropriate.

First, this blueprint has selected a 10-year schedule. If debt retirement bonds are to be issued in January 1994, the initial payment on principal and debt service would be made in December 1994, and the final payment in December 2003. A Plan with a longer schedule could be formulated with minor adjustments. With a longer repayment schedule the Plan would require a lower tax rate, but the aggregate service costs would increase in proportion to the number of years the debt retirement bonds are to be carried. Interest bearing bonds will be issued with ten different maturity dates, commencing December 1994 and extending through December 2003.

Second, debt retirement bonds issued in January 1994 have an estimated value of $4.03 trillion. This is derived by analyzing the value of outstanding federal debt securities in mid-July 1992, which totaled just over $4 trillion.[7] The outstanding debt securities are held by both private investors, $2.9 trillion, and by U.S. government agencies and trust funds, $1.1 trillion. The Plan proposes to exchange debt retirement bonds on an equal value, or one-for-one, basis for the outstanding debt held by federal agencies and trust funds. The exchange for the privately held securities builds in an incentive. Private bond holders could then trade their outstanding debt for debt retirement bonds of comparable maturities at a 1 percent premium. For example, bond holders could exchange outstanding securities worth $1 million for debt retirement bonds worth $1,010,000. Upon completion of the exchange $1.1 trillion in debt retirement bonds would be held by federal agencies and trusts funds and $2.933 trillion by private investors.

Third, the interest rates on the debt retirement bonds are calculated to approximate the average interest rates on outstanding debt securities of comparable maturity. Again, it is assumed that comparable rates are required to attract private investors to exchange outstanding debt for the new issues (plus the 1 percent premium already noted). The amount of debt retirement bonds issued at each maturity and the interest rates are shown in Table 10-2.

TABLE 10-2
STRUCTURE OF DEBT RETIREMENT BONDS

	Trillion
Total Value of Debt Retirement Bonds:*	$4.033
Retirement Bonds Held by Private Investors:	$2.933
Retirement Bonds Held by U.S. Government Agencies and Trust Funds:	$1.100

Year of Maturity	Interest Rate at Offering	Amount Issued at Each Maturity (in Billions)	Percent of National Debt Retired
1994	5.00%	$169.6	4.2%
1995	5.50%	$206.3	9.3%
1996	5.75%	$247.5	15.5%
1997	6.00%	$293.4	22.7%
1998	6.50%	$344.5	31.3%
1999	7.00%	$402.5	41.3%
2000	7.50%	$468.3	52.9%
2001	8.00%	$543.4	66.4%
2002	8.50%	$629.3	82.0%
2003	9.00%	$727.6	100.0%

Total Issue = $4,032.5

*Notes: Private debt that must be exchanged is $2.90 billion. Public debt that must be exchanged is $1.10 billion. Assumes a premium of 1.1 percent would be needed to make the exchange attractive to private investors and that government debt would be exchanged one-for-one.

Fourth, this Plan assumes that tax revenues are collected by applying a uniform tax rate to the revenue base for each year, as projected in Table 10-1, and that a constant tax rate is established and applied throughout the full 10-year period. An alternative to a constant tax rate would be to phase-in the tax, using lower rates in the earlier years with gradual increases in succeeding periods. The potential advantage of phasing-in the dedicated tax would be to reduce the adverse consequences on prices and output until the positive effects from debt reduction have a chance to boost economic growth. As the growth effects of the Plan begin to materialize and the economy expands, gradually increasing tax rates would be less disruptive. The disadvantage of phasing-in tax rates is to increase interest costs. A longer maturity structure for the bond portfolio would be required because less revenue would be available in the initial years.

These assumptions, parameters, and economic projections are the predicate for selecting the term structure and total issue of the debt retirement bonds that are displayed in Table 10-2. An 8.6 percent tax rate is required to generate sufficient revenue flows to service the debt retirement bonds and totally repay the principal in 10 years.[8]

COMMENTARY

The details of how the payments are applied annually toward the repayment of principal and the costs of interest are furnished in Table 10-3.

TABLE 10-3
PATH TO DEBT RETIREMENT: DISBURSEMENTS OF DEDICATED TAX REVENUES

Year	Payment on Principal (Billions)	Annual Interest (Billions)	Outstanding Principal (Trillions)
1994	$169.6	$300	$3.9
1995	206.3	291	3.7
1996	247.5	280	3.4
1997	293.4	266	3.1
1998	344.5	248	2.8
1999	402.5	226	2.4
2000	468.3	198	1.9
2001	543.4	162	1.4
2002	629.3	119	0.7
2003	727.6	65	0.0

Notes: Initial principal borrowed would be $4.033 trillion.

For example the 8.6 percent tax rate generates $469.4 billion in revenues in the first year of the Plan (1994). Of this amount, $169.6 billion is applied to retiring the principal on the 1 year bonds and $299.8 billion is applied to paying the interest charges.

The application of the tax revenues as between principal and interest costs adjusts in accordance with the scheduled payments of the debt retirement bonds. Importantly, the interest costs as a share of the annual payment declines at an increasing rate. In the first year, the interest costs account for 63 percent of that annual payment; by 2003, the last year, interest costs account for 8 only percent. The crossover point will occur in the fourth year, 1997, when 52 percent of the payment goes toward retiring the outstanding principal and 48 percent toward the interest costs.

The accelerating decline in debt service costs is an important illustration of how the tyranny of compound interest can be harnessed once the principal amount of the national debt begins to be reduced. The federal government has continued to run deficits and to refund the past debt, and by this practice interest costs have grown at an increasing rate. But by the same token, interest costs shrink exponentially as the Plan outlined here operates to reduce the debt's outstanding balance. More than half the national debt is retired by the close of the year 2000, 7 years after the initiation of the Plan. From there it takes only 3 more years to finish the job.

An 8.6 percent consumption tax might have adverse economic consequences in the absence of a reduction in other taxes to provide offsetting compensation. Specifically a reduction in income taxes or payroll taxes or a combination of the two should be effected for this purpose.

The Debt Retirement Plan is designed to correct decades of fiscal profligacy that has left the nation on the brink of bankruptcy. The Plan requires structural changes in the present fiscal program and adjustments in the form of reduced consumption in the short term. Beliefs that a solution to the nation's debt problem will one day be discovered that does not require sacrifices, or that the debt will simply go away, is an insidious formula for national decay approaching with an ever accelerating pace. The choice is plain: America must act to adopt a fundamentally different fiscal structure or a solution ultimately will be imposed by the transcendent force of those circumstances Americans refused to resolve.

NOTES

[1]With all its good intentions to achieve a balanced budget by 1990, the road for the Gramm-Rudman Balanced Budget Act of 1986 was one continuous minefield. The absence of an unbreachable enforcement mechanism meant that deficit targets and deadlines set in the original Gramm-Rudman legislation were amended time and again. The "budget balance-by-1990" goal was an historical failure, nor could have it have been expected to be otherwise. Congress and the administration were not irrevocably committed to any specific program ethically or otherwise.

[2]As further evidence of the unwillingness of incumbent politicians to breach contracts with lenders, we need only witness the behavior of the U.S. state governments. In contrast to the looming deficits at the federal level, state governments ran surpluses throughout the decade of the 1980s. The difference is that state governments lack the power to "print money" and generally resort to private credit markets, if current expenditures exceed revenues. In essence, fiscal management at the state level is "policed" by current and potential creditors. Should mismanagement of a state's budget arise, credit markets provide an immediate signal that is easily monitored by voters and lenders.

[3]President William Clinton had come forward early in his term with a program for large tax increases on a broad scale. That kind of suggestion does not naturally find popular response. Coupled with the assorted statements of a contrary vein with which he had punctuated his successful presidential campaign of 1992, a different expectation about taxes may have been aroused.

Against this backdrop President Clinton seemed to have found a need for greater public confidence, and he proposed a "deficit-reduction trust fund". New tax revenues and savings from purported reductions of present programs would then be used to reduce the deficit. This "Clinton trust" appeared to have the aspects of a binding committment for deficit reduction. However, the "Clinton trust" in contrast to the Debt Retirement Plan, carried with it no binding or enforceable consequences. Actually it would not restrict government spending. Indeed the Clinton administration's deputy director of OMB labeled this a "display device". And for so long as such spending exceeeds federal revenue, as it did under President Clinton's first budget, growth of the national debt would continue.

See *The New York Times*, May 13, 1993, "Clinton Supports Creating Fund Designated Soley to Cut Deficit," A1; see also *The Wall Street Journal*, May 13, 1993, "Clinton Ties Any New Tax Revenues and Program Savings to Cutting Deficit," A2.

[4]The payroll tax dedicated to financing future payments covered by the social security system has built up an apparent multibillion dollar surplus. The accumulating surplus of social security funds in current periods is needed because liabilities in future periods (beginning about 2010) are projected to be much greater than receipts. More citizens will qualify for social security benefits by the second decade of the twenty-first century than there will be payees into the system. Thus, current surpluses are necessary to make the system actuarially solvent. However, because all temporary surpluses in the social security system must be invested only in U.S. government securities, the budget deficit in the non-social security components of the budget appears smaller than it otherwise would be. One part of the federal budget is effectively borrowing from another. A by-product of this temporary reduction in the government's deficit is an incentive to increase spending, or at least to deter deficit reduction in other parts of the federal budget. Social security surpluses are ephemeral and not "saved", but as they are converted into the general receipts they tend to fuel higher current federal spending, and the future net liability of the federal government rises.

[5]Each type of security has a comparative advantage and disadvantage, and a mix of the two maturity characteristics is probably the best solution. Government bonds with non-extendible maturity dates would result in a lower interest cost than bonds with extendible maturities. The option to

extend simply adds a degree of uncertainty, and potential investors demand an interest "premium" to compensate for this added risk. Issuing refinancing bonds with flexible maturity dates, while more expensive in terms of interest costs, has a key advantage. Given a revenue shortfall in one fiscal period, repayment can be extended to the next period and the need for future political action to increase the dedicated tax is averted. A mixed debt portfolio of extendible and non-extendible securities gains some of the advantages of both: the lower interest requirements of fixed maturity bonds and the ability of the Plan to self-adjust and operate independently.

[6]Imposition of a consumption tax dedicated to financing the debt retirement bonds may be politically indigestible. Steps can be taken, however, to make it more palatable. For example, reduction or elimination of the federal income tax could be linked to the imposition of the dedicated consumption tax. Elimination of the income tax would clearly resolve controversy over taxes on capital gains: there would be no such tax at all. Other possibilities include a reduction in the social security payroll tax tied to enactment of the dedicated consumption tax. In general, policies that exchange a tax on production for a tax on consumption would be growth-promoting.

[7]*Monthly Statement of the Public Debt*, July 31, 1992 and CBO, *The Economic and Budget Outlook: An Update*, August 1992. Note that $3.66 trillion is the size of the *gross debt*, which includes debt held by federal agencies and trust funds. *Net debt*, which is discussed at other points in this book, includes only debt held by private investors.

[8]The solution for the amount of debt to be issued at each maturity and the tax rate is a linear optimization problem. An intuitive way to think about the problem is to ask: what is the minimum tax rate required to generate annual tax revenues to repay the $4.03 trillion borrowed in 1994 at the interest rates postulated for each maturity? The flow of revenues available in each period under alternative tax rates are

known given the estimated size of the tax base (from Table 10-1). The payments due in each period under alternative scenarios about the amount of debt issued at each maturity are known given the interest rates specified in Table 10-2. Given these two computations, the linear optimization procedure solves simultaneously the bond allocation and the minimum tax rate requirement.

11

Epilogue:
Present Choices and
Future Expectations

PARADISE LOST

We have now arrived at the year 2004. The national elections are in full bloom and the incoming administration will inherit a projected $690 billion budget deficit in fiscal year 2005 (see Figure 11-1).[1] In the midst of the campaign the national debt held by the public reached a grim milestone: at $10.6 trillion it had just surpassed America's GDP (see Figure 11-2). Interest payments on the debt are $800 billion, accounting for 30 percent of the entire federal budget (see Figure 11-1).

Then along about 1995 enlarging problems in financing the federal deficit began to appear. The report that the Congressional Budget Office (CBO) sent to the Congress in August of 1992 forecast that the deficit would recede to about $244 billion in fiscal year 1995 and that the national debt would be $3.8 trillion. This was wildly optimistic. The recession, then extant, restrained economic recovery, and the presumed extraordinary expenditure to resolve the thrift crisis was succeeded by other crises: in health care and the clean-up of nuclear waste sites in both the United States and the former Soviet Union. Federal spending growth did not

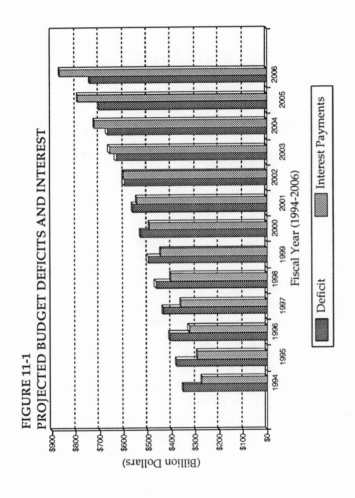

FIGURE 11-1
PROJECTED BUDGET DEFICITS AND INTEREST

Fiscal Year (1994-2006)

Deficit   Interest Payments

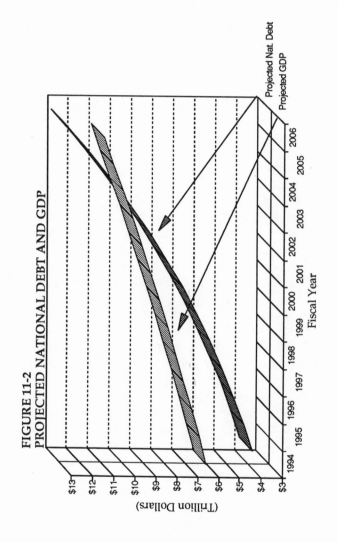

FIGURE 11-2
PROJECTED NATIONAL DEBT AND GDP

Projected Nat. Debt

Projected GDP

Fiscal Year

(Trillion Dollars)

$13
$12
$11
$10
$9
$8
$7
$6
$5
$4
$3

1994 1995 1996 1997 1998 1999 2000 2001 2002 2003 2004 2005 2006

decline as the administration and Congressional forecasters had claimed. The deficit turned out to be $390 billion, almost double the officially projected level. Consequently, larger debt obligations had to be sold to finance the revenue shortfalls and more interest had to be paid. Interest on the debt was nearly $300 billion in fiscal year 1995, 20 percent higher than the $244 billion that CBO had projected in 1992.

This condition put additional pressure on the financial markets as the government's demand for domestic and foreign savings increased. The Federal Reserve's continued effort to revive the sluggish economy through monetary policy eventually increased apprehension of debt monetization and future inflation. These drove long-term borrowing costs still higher. Business activity began to slacken and unemployment rose. Consequently, tax revenues receded but federal expenditures on entitlements to support the unemployed increased. Continued resistance to any tax increase remained unrelenting. Interest costs to service the debt continued to rise, and Treasury borrowings accelerated. Selling these issues required higher interest rates to attract buyers.

Rates required to sell long-term securities in the Treasury auctions of early 1996 reached 14 percent, a level not seen since the Carter period 20 years earlier. The Treasury finally abandoned any further effort to sell long term obligations. Future offerings were of 5 year maturity or less and even these required rates of at least 10 percent to be saleable. Schemes were put forth to pay interest in kind or exchange Treasury bonds for new zero-coupon issues.

In fiscal year 1997 debt held by the public had become $5.2 trillion, having risen from $3.5 trillion in 1992, a period of only 5 years. Annual interest payments on the debt were $362 billion in 1997, up 80 percent from $201 billion in 1992. The downward economic trend accelerated under this heavy debt load, and the inflationary fears in 1995 turned out to be justified. Efforts to monetize the debt were intensifying, and 1997 witnessed price increases that measured inflation at 13 percent. A move to print money and eliminate a portion of the debt was high on the political agenda. The monetization of the debt was the least unpalatable way to repudiate the debt and lift even temporarily its crushing burden on the nation's financial and industrial structure. It was against ethical principles but survival was paramount. The angle of economic decline steepened.

In January 2002 privately held debt had risen to $8 trillion, nearly doubling in a decade. The federal budget that was submitted to Congress then showed interest costs to be just under $600 billion, and by coincidence the federal deficit was projected to hit $600 billion. Shortly thereafter the U.S. Treasury tried to auction $100 billion of new debt obligations. The offering failed, and the most easily adaptable option was to pay off creditors by printing dollars. The inflationary consequences were obvious to the World, interest rates soared with severe damage to the financial integrity of the United States government.

In desperation the president announced America's plan to delay interest payments and obligations on maturing Treasury securities held by non-citizens of the United States for a period of 2 years (until after the 2004 election). Outraged foreign creditors demanded radical United States fiscal restructuring, including tax increases and across the board spending cuts to reduce the debt. United States compliance was a condition precedent to participation by foreign lenders in further financing of America's debt. These conditions were reminiscent of those imposed by the United States on Third World countries in the 1980s and 1990s. The precise terms for the reform would be dictated and overseen by a special task force appointed by the World Bank. A familiar refrain was sounded, but this time for the United States of America: failure to submit to the World Bank task force recommendations would result in a suspension of foreign lending to the public and private institutions in the United States. Seizure of all assets abroad was also dictated to provide collateral until the debt payments were resumed.

Authority over our destiny and unfettered exercise of our sovereignty became dependent upon the consent of foreign powers. Failing to resolve the national debt problem by our own determination, the new rules for fiscal discipline were written and enforced by the economic powers in the global community.

PARADISE REGAINED: CHOICES OF SELF-INTEREST

Looking at the past, the fiscal behavior and economic facts lead inexorably to an outlook far from attractive. The projections are based on straightforward forecasting techniques. The extrapolations that were drawn from patterns developed in the absence of a plan for debt retirement suggest an unpleasant future for America.

The opportunity for free choice of solutions is rapidly diminishing. A financial situation in which the national debt grows more rapidly than the country's ability to pay cannot go on indefinitely. Either the debt must be retired by a self-determined plan or it will be repudiated through the pursuit of policies discussed in this book. If it were likely that the country will soon find itself on a path leading to debt retirement, this book would have been written with a different exposition. The course of events foretells with a considerable degree of confidence that America's political leaders will eschew debt repayment and rush full speed ahead down the road to repudiation. This choice is not inevitable, and lessons from the distant past offer a glimmer of hope that with responsible leadership America's financial integrity can be preserved. But without immediate political action to invoke a debt retirement plan the final possibility to avoid financial collapse will be lost.

America is in a vicious circle because sluggish income growth has provided the motivation for families to save less and borrow more in an effort to maintain living standards. The catch is that a low savings rate makes it harder to increase living standards. Figure 11-3 illustrates the pattern of real disposable income per capita since 1962, and the future path that is projected under the current fiscal regime. Between 1962 and 1976 this indicator of living standards grew by nearly 50 percent, with an average yearly growth rate of

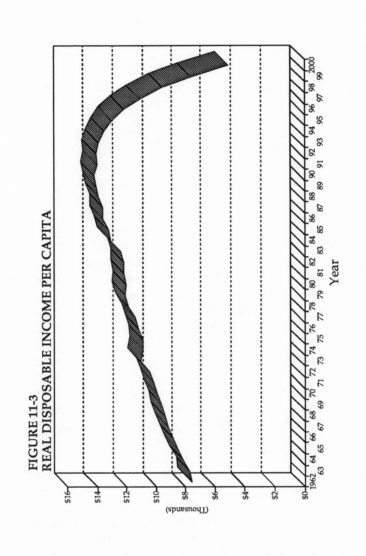

FIGURE 11-3
REAL DISPOSABLE INCOME PER CAPITA

3.4 percent. During the administrations of Carter, Reagan, and Bush (1977 through 1993) real disposable income grew at an average yearly rate of only 1.4 percent. This drop from a 3.4 percent to a 1.4 percent growth rate actually understates that magnitude of the problem. In fact the *rate of change* in the growth of disposable income began to decline in the mid-1970s and is projected to turn negative in the mid-1990s as Figure 11-3 illustrates. When this changing pattern in the growth rate is accounted for in the time-series forecasts, real disposable income at the turn of the century is projected to be less than half of what it was in 1991.

When a plan for elimination of the debt is pursued the path to a healthy state of economic growth and prosperity is possible. Then hundreds of billions of dollars in debt servicing costs will no longer be siphoned from the pool of family savings. Figure 11-4 illustrates the declining national debt that would occur assuming the Debt Retirement Plan is implemented in 1994. Figure 11-5 shows the interest costs associated with the Plan, as outlined in Chapter 10.

The Debt Retirement Plan embodies the extraordinary measures required for successful removal of the most formidable obstacle to America's prosperity. The Plan rechannels excessive consumption spending into productive capital investments. Interest rates, no longer bloated and volatile from the constant pressure of federal borrowing, will create a fertile financial environment for investment to flourish. Enacting the dedicated tax and pursuing the elimination of the costs of federal debt service will make it possible to lower tax rates in the future.

The full impact of the Debt Retirement Plan will take several years to materialize as new investments come on stream and begin to increase the productivity of American workers. But even in the near term, the slide in living standards can be halted. The projected figures indicate a dramatic decline under the present course of inaction on the debt, and this must be reversed before an era of renewed prosperity can take hold. Compared to the accelerating decline in living standards as projected, even a small positive

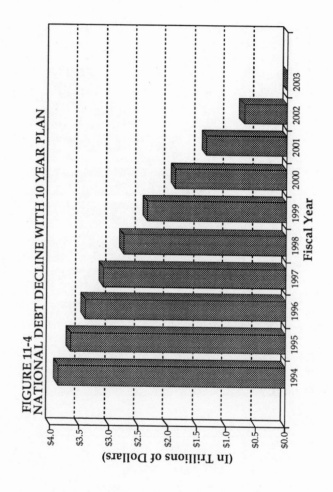

FIGURE 11-4
NATIONAL DEBT DECLINE WITH 10 YEAR PLAN

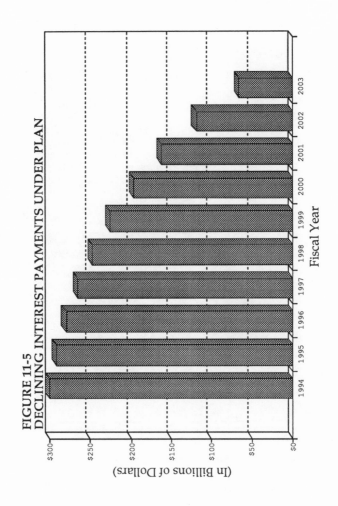

FIGURE 11-5
DECLINING INTEREST PAYMENTS UNDER PLAN

growth rate should be welcomed. The Plan is designed to retire the debt over a 10 year period and as the debt is eliminated the growth rate in living standards will accordingly increase.

Suppose the Plan is implemented in 1994 and living standards experience no further decline for the next 5 years and then return to the 3.4 percent growth of the 1962 to 1976 period. In the year 2000 real income per person would be $9,800 higher than it would be given the projected levels under the status quo.

The outlook for the longer term will be enhanced as the sinews of the Debt Retirement Plan work their way through the economy and restore confidence in America's financial management. Freedom from that great millstone that drags down the creation of new productive assets will be a reality. The degenerating power of the federal debt that is immobilizing the economy will be replaced by the rejuvenating force of capital accumulation and national determination.

NOTE

[1]The methodology used to forecast long-term fiscal and economic conditions is described in the Appendix.

Appendix:
Forecasting Methodology

The forecasts for the various fiscal and economic variables in Chapter 11 use historical data starting with 1962. Two forms of conventional forecasting techniques are employed: time-series models and econometric models.

Time-series models observe the past behavior of a variable, for example, federal expenditures from 1962 through 1993, and extrapolate into the future based on the observed systematic patterns. These patterns might be some kind of overall upward or downward trend in the data, or a kind of cyclical behavior. On this basis a time-series model accounts for patterns in the past movements of a particular variable, and uses that information to predict future movements in the variable. Econometric models predict future movements in a variable by relating it to a set of other variables in a causal framework. For example, interest payments to service the debt depend on the size of the past and present federal debt. Projected future interest payments are thus related to the projected behavior of debt. The methodology used for each forecast is described later.[1]

GROSS DOMESTIC PRODUCT (GDP)

GDP forecasts are obtained using an integrated autoregressive moving average model (ARIMA model) for time series. The GDP data series is stationary after second-differencing (i.e., a second-order homogeneous process), which is a basic requirement for an unbiased ARIMA estimation. The best fit for the historical GDP time-series pattern is represented by a first-order moving average process and a first-order autoregressive process. This means that projected changes in the growth pattern of GDP has a "memory" of the current change in GDP growth and the change in GDP growth in one past period. The technically trained reader will recognize the designation of the GDP forecasting equation as an ARIMA(1,2,1) model.

FEDERAL DEBT

The most accurate forecasts were obtained by estimating an ARIMA(1,2,1) time-series model (as described for GDP) using the 1962 to 1993 data series for federal debt as a percentage of GDP. The projected *levels* for the future federal debt were then obtained by multiplying this percentage by the GDP forecasts.

FEDERAL DEFICIT

The federal deficit projections were computed by first forecasting future values of federal revenues and federal expenditures and then taking the difference. ARIMA(1,2,1) time-series models for expenditures and revenues were estimated using the 1962 through 1993 data.

INTEREST PAYMENTS ON THE DEBT

An econometric model was used to forecast the future interest costs. The model that yielded the smallest forecasting error (a generally accepted criterion for evaluating such models) specified a relationship between interest costs as a percentage of federal expenditures and federal debt as a percentage of GDP. The regression equation included federal debt in current and previous fiscal years as independent variables. The projected *level* of future interest payments were then obtained by multiplying the values for interest as a percentage of federal expenditures times the projected levels of Federal expenditures. (The model used to produce projections on federal expenditures is described under the FEDERAL DEFICIT section.)

REAL DISPOSABLE PERSONAL INCOME PER CAPITA

An ARIMA(3,2,1) time-series model was employed to forecast future values for real disposable personal income per capita. In this case the data series is second-differenced and the order of the moving-average process is 1. The smallest forecasting errors were obtained with a model that allowed for a third-order autoregressive process (i.e., a three period "memory" of past changes in the income variable).

NOTE

[1]See Pindyck and Rubinfeld (1981), pp. 469–573 for a detailed description of the forecasting techniques. All statistical models are estimated using *Shazam*, Version 6.2.

Bibliography

Adams, Henry C., *Public Debts* (New York: Arno Press), 1975.

Anderson, Gary A., "The U.S. Federal Deficit and National Debt: Political and Economic History," in Buchanan, J.M., Rowley C.K., and Tollison, R.D. (eds), *Deficits* (Basil Blackwell), 1986.

Bastable, Charles F., *Public Finance* (London and New York: The MacMillan Co.), 1892.

Blinder, Alan and Robert Solow, "Does Fiscal Policy Matter?" *Journal of Public Economics*, 2 (November 1973), pp. 319-337.

Bollas, Albert Sydney, *The Financial History of the U.S. from 1861 to 1885* (New York: D. Appleton and Co.), 1886.

Bowen, William G., Richard G. Davis, and David Kopf, "The Public Debt: A Burden on Future Generations," in James Ferguson (ed.), *The Public Debt and Future Generations* (Chapel Hill, NC: University of North Carolina Press), 1964.

Buchanan, James M., "Public Debt and Capital Formation," in Dwight Lee (ed.), *Taxation and the Deficit Economy* (San Francisco: Pacific Research Institute for Public Policy), 1986.

Buchanan, James M., and Herbert Stein, *The Fiscal Revolution in America* (Chicago: University of Chicago Press), 1967.

Bureau of Labor Statistics, cited in "Harper's Index" *Harper's* (September 1986).

Bureau of the Census, Historical Statistics of the U.S.: *Colonial Times to 1970* (Washington, DC: U.S. Government Printing Office), 1970.

Committee on Public Debt Policy, *Our National Debt* (New York: Harcourt, Brace and Co., Inc.) 1949.

Committee on the Judiciary, U.S. Senate, *Amendments to the Constitution: A Brief Legislative History* (Washington, DC: U.S. Government Printing Office), October 1985.

"Conversion of the National Debt to Capital," *Lippincott's Monthly Magazine*, I (June 1868).

Council of Economic Advisers, *The Economic Report of the President*, 1987 and 1992.

Courant, Paul and Edward Gramlich, *Federal Budget Deficits: America's Consumption Binge* (Englewood Cliffs, NJ: Prentice Hall), 1986.

Day, Kathleen, "With Debt Burgeoning, Could the U.S. Default?" *Washington Post*, June 14, 1992.

Evans, Michael, *The Truth About Supply-Side Economics* (New York: Basic Books), 1983.

Federal Reserve Bulletin, March 1946.

Grace Commission, *Report* (Washington, DC: U.S. Government Printing Office), 1984.

Gray, Thomas, "Elegy Written in a Country Church-Yard," in *Gray Poetry and Prose* (London: Oxford University Press), 1963.

Groves, Harold M., *Financing Government*, 6th ed. (New York: Holt Rinehart and Winston), 1964.

Hepburn, Barton A., *History of Coinage and Currency in the United States and the Perennial Contest for Sound Money* (New York and London: The MacMillan Co.), 1903.

Hershey, Robert D., Jr., "Why Economists Fear the Deficit," *The New York Times*, May 27, 1992.

Keynes, John Maynard, *A Tract on Monetary Reform* (London: The MacMillan Co.), 1923.

Kotlikoff, L., "Economic Impact of Deficit Finance," *IMF Staff Papers*, Vol. 31, September 1984.

Lerner, Alan C., "The Truth about the 'D' Word," *The Washington Post*, April 22, 1992.

McCulloch, Hugh, *Men and Measures of Half a Century* (New York: Charles Scribner's & Son), 1888.

Monthly Statement of the Public Debt, July 31, 1992 and CBO, *The Economic and Budget Outlook: An Update*, August 1992.

Myers, Margaret G., *A Financial History of the United States* (New York: Columbia University Press), 1970.

"National Health Expenditures, 1986-2000," *Health Care Financing Review*, No. 8, Summer 1987.

National Journal, February 22, 1992.

Pascall, Glenn, *The Trillion Dollar Budget* (Seattle: University of Washington Press), 1985.

Patterson, Robert, *Federal Debt Management Policies, 1865-1879* (Durham, NC: Duke University Press), 1954.

Pindyck, R. and D. Rubinfeld, *Econometric Models and Economic Forecasts* (New York: McGraw-Hill), 1981.

Pollock v. Farmers' Loan and Trust Company, 157 U.S. 429 (1895) and 158 U.S. 601 (1895).

Prestowitz, Clyde V., *Trading Places* (New York: Basic Books), 1989.

Report of the Comptroller of the Currency, 1865.

Rosen, Harvey, "Housing Decisions and the U.S. Income Tax: An Econometric Analysis," *Journal of Public Economics*, 11 (February 1979).

Ross, Edward A., "Sinking Funds," *Publications of the American Economic Association*, First Series, 1892, Vol. VII, Nos. 4-5.

The London Economist, XXIV (Dec. 22, 1866).

Tolchin, Martin and Susan Tolchin, "Foreign Money, U.S. Fears," *New York Times Sunday Magazine* (December 13, 1897), p. 63.

Treasury Report, 1865 and 1866.

U.S. Bureau of the Census, Current Population Reports, Series P-20, No. 363, *Population Profile of the United States, 1980* (Washington, DC: U.S. Government Printing Office), 1981.

Walker, Francis, A., "The National Debt," *Lippincott's Monthly Magazine*, IV (September 1869).

Index

About the Author

CHARLES W. STEADMAN is an attorney and financier specializing in corporate finance, private banking, and capital investment. He is chairman of Steadman Security Corporation, a private bank in Washington, D.C., and chairman of the National Debt Repayment Foundation, also in Washington.